# 52 Reasons to Vote for

Bernard Whitman

Brittany L. Stalsburg, PhD

PRESS

WESTPORT AND NEW YORK

Published by Prospecta Press, an imprint of Easton Studio Press
P.O. Box 3131
Westport, CT 06880
(203) 571-0781
www.prospectapress.com

Designed by Barbara Aronica-Buck for Booktrix

First Edition
Manufactured in the United States of America
Trade paperback ISBN: 978-1-63226-071-0
eBook ISBN: 978-1-63226-072-7

To my two grandmothers—Grace Stalsburg, the original "boss babe," and the reason why politics is in my blood; and Violet DeLano—my Italian grandmother, another boss babe who gave me my moxie.

—BLS

To my mom and dad, Gerda and Nelson Whitman, who instilled a love of politics in me from a very early age, taught me right from wrong, and never wavered in their support.

—BW

# Contents

## III. Human Dignity

## IV. Freedom

# Acknowledgments

We wrote this book during one of the busiest years in both of our lives. Brittany planned a wedding and got married and Bernard oversaw one of the biggest growth spurts in his company's history. In the midst of this whirlwind we also decided it would be a good idea to write a book about Hillary Clinton. It almost didn't happen several times, but it did, and there are many people we need to thank who helped push this book forward.

First we'd like to thank everyone at Whitman Insight Strategies who not only covered for us when we were busy writing and editing, but who provided valuable feedback and support for this project throughout the process. We'd like to thank the interns who helped with the research for this book among other important tasks, especially Maya Daver-Massion. We are very grateful to Ross Aaron, our dedicated book intern, whose excellent research and analysis provided the foundation we needed to write a compelling story about Hillary.

Thank you to the team at Prospecta Press, especially David Wilk, who helped propel this book forward and provided exceptional advice along the way.

Thank you to our family and friends and our partners: Constantin Mitides and Chuck Fritch. We could not have done this, or anything else, without your loving support and encouragement.

— Bernard Whitman
and Brittany L. Stalsburg,
June 2016

# Introduction

Hillary Clinton has occupied the political spotlight for more than three decades—as First Lady of Arkansas, First Lady of the United States, US Senator from New York, 2008 presidential candidate, and secretary of state. Her professional and personal lives have been analyzed, scrutinized, and criticized incessantly, as she has been the subject of thousands of articles, stories, books, and dinnertime debates.

Despite the fact that Hillary has been in the public eye for decades, a common refrain is that Hillary herself is, in many ways, unknown. The established storyline is that Hillary is aloof, secretive, and inaccessible. This reputation has hurt her in the eyes of voters who yearn more than ever for a leader who seems authentic and in touch with the concerns of American families.

This book seeks to re-introduce Hillary to America and re-tell her story, not only as an experienced, accomplished public servant, but also her life as a real person—a daughter, wife, mother, grandmother, and role model for women and girls around the world.

We, the authors of this book, are lifelong Democrats and strong Hillary supporters. We wrote this book not only to convince our readers to vote for Hillary, but also to re-educate America about who Hillary is and what she is about. With so much misinformation and exaggeration swirling around, it is critical that we tell readers the facts about Hillary Clinton.

So what does Hillary stand for? After we examined her forty-year record as a public servant as well as her personal life history, we concluded that Hillary stands for five core values: Opportunity, Fairness, Respect for Human Dignity, Freedom, and Perseverance. The story we tell in this book is centered on how Hillary's actions and plans for the future reflect those five values.

Hillary believes that every American should have the opportunity to live up to their potential, and that we must do all we can to knock down barriers that hold Americans back from getting ahead and staying ahead. Here we talk about Hillary's plans to create jobs, and highlight some of her proposals to eliminate obstacles to economic opportunity, such as her strategy to increase college affordability and her plan to ensure working parents don't have to choose between a paycheck and childcare.

We begin the Fairness section detailing Hillary's plan to create an economy that is fair for all Americans, which is at the core of her campaign. Hillary has also proposed reforming the criminal justice system, ensuring equal pay for women, and building on the progress President Obama has made in providing healthcare access for all Americans.

Respect for the human dignity of all people has been a cornerstone of Hillary's vision for America and the world. She has spent her career fighting for human rights around the globe, dating back to 1995 when she proclaimed in Beijing that women's rights are human rights. She has been an advocate for marginalized groups and is committed to ensuring that no American is left behind. Hillary will fight for the rights of immigrants, people of color, women, LGBT people, seniors, veterans, the disabled, and those who suffer from mental health and substance abuse issues. Hillary's America is one where it doesn't matter what you look like or where you come from, but what you contribute to your community and country that makes you American.

Freedom is a core American value, and one that Hillary will defend, protect, and preserve as President of the United States. Hillary's foreign policy experience equips her well to restore American leadership around the world and aggressively protect the United States from foreign threats like ISIS. She will be ready on day one to take on the role of commander in chief, and has both the strength and the smarts to lead the free world. In this section, we also discuss Hillary's commitment to ensuring a balance between security and privacy, as well as her lifelong commitment to protecting women's reproductive freedom.

Hillary has said that although she's been called many things in her life, a quitter is not one of them. The Perseverance section is an ode to that sentiment, and details Hillary's relentless efforts and lifelong commitment to being a champion for American families. It is in this section that we re-tell some of Hillary's earlier life history, including her roots in the Midwest, her relationship with her mother, and the story of how she turned Bill down—twice!—before she agreed to marry him. We also detail Hillary's exceptional record of bringing people together and compromising to get things done for American families.

We believe that by the end of this book, the reader will come away with a wealth of knowledge to articulate why Hillary is the candidate who will bring America forward, into the twenty-first century, and will ensure that no American gets left behind. While the Republicans want to roll back the progress our country has made and return to the past, Hillary knows that America's best days are ahead. America has always been great—the task now is to bring Americans together and make us whole, and that is exactly what Hillary Clinton will do as President of the United States.

*Please visit our website for updates and timely news about the election: www.52ReasonsToVoteForHillary.com.*

# 52 Reasons to Vote for Hillary

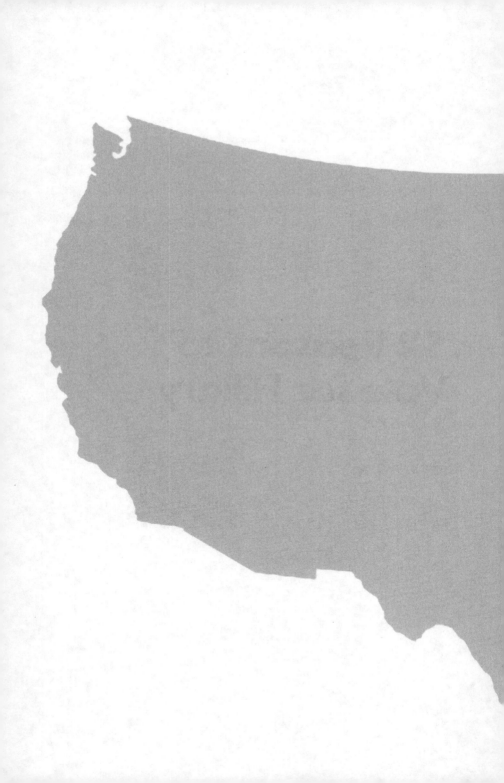

# Opportunity

# 1  She Is Looking Toward the Future, Not the Past

*"I'm running for president to build an America for tomorrow, not yesterday, an America built on growth and fairness, an America where if you do your part, you will reap the rewards, where we don't leave anyone behind."*
—Hillary Clinton[1]

As president, Hillary will bring this country forward, into a brighter future that doesn't leave anyone behind. Her vision for a twenty-first-century America is about knocking down barriers, ensuring that all Americans everywhere have access to opportunities, and respecting the dignity of every human being. Hillary wants to build the America of tomorrow, the country that we want our children and grandchildren to inherit. In contrast, the Republicans want to bring our country backward—with failed economic policies that benefit the wealthy and big corporations, and with social policies that resemble the rules of the 1950s and promote intolerance and even hatred. The choice in this election is about what Americans want their country to look like in the twenty-first century, and whether we want to move our country forward into the future or backward into the past.

The core of Hillary's vision involves creating an economy for tomorrow. Thanks to President Obama, our country has made tremendous progress toward economic recovery, but we're not at the point where families can get ahead and stay ahead. From day one, Hillary's priority will be to raise incomes for American families. Her plan is to build an economy that is strong, fair, and sustainable for the long-term. Hillary opposes the economic plans espoused by Republicans, including those who want to lower taxes for the wealthy and big corporations and roll back consumer protections that hold Wall Street accountable. Their economic proposals cling to ideas that have already been tried and have failed, yet Republicans keep insisting that we go back to the past.[2] As Hillary explains the difference between her economic vision and the vision of Republicans:

"Fundamentally, they reject what it takes to build an inclusive economy. It takes an inclusive society. What I once called 'a village' that has a place for everyone."[3]

Hillary will bring America forward in the social policy realm as well. The Republicans want to roll back the incredible progress our country has made in advancing the rights of women, LGBT people, and people of color. They want to go back to the days when women did not have the right to make their own reproductive health decisions, when marriage was defined as only between a man and a woman, and when racist rhetoric was tolerated. Hillary wants to build a different America, one that is built on the values of opportunity, fairness, freedom, and respect for the human dignity of all people.

Hillary's America will be one where every American has an equal chance to succeed in our great country; where the economy works for American families, not just billionaires and CEOs; where all Americans can live their lives without fear of discrimination, gun violence, or a terrorist attack; and where women, LGBT individuals, immigrants, and people of color are afforded the respect they deserve. This is the country of the future, and Hillary will be the leader who takes us there. It's our time.

# 2 ➤ She Is a Woman

*"It is past time for women to take their rightful place, side by side with men, in the rooms where the fates of peoples, where their children's and grandchildren's fates, are decided."*

—Hillary Clinton[1]

The election of Hillary Rodham Clinton to the highest office in our country will be a game-changer for America. Not only will the election of the first woman president be a historic signal of equality, but it will also have profound effects on American society, including increased attention to issues that affect working families and tens of millions of Americans.

The visibility of women leaders—especially at the executive level—has a significant "role model" effect on younger women and girls.[2] Simply put, *seeing* a woman occupy the highest position of power in the United States sends the message that they too can be president of the United States, or anything else for that matter. Visible women leaders empower women and can encourage more women to seek leadership roles.

More women at all levels of office—from the presidency to city councils—is good for our country. Of course, it's not just having different body parts that make women act differently from men as leaders; it's gender, and how women and men are socialized in our society.[3] On average, women have different life experiences than men. For example, they are still more likely to be the primary caregivers to children and elderly relatives,[4] have different health needs and concerns,[5] are more likely to live in poverty,[6] and make up the vast majority of rape survivors.[7] Different experiences mean different perspectives, and in today's political world, new voices at the table are desperately needed.

Research provides evidence that women leaders do indeed act differently from men. For one, the *way* in which they govern is different: they are more likely to build consensus and collaborate—

leadership styles that might actually help fix the gridlock and dysfunction that characterize our broken political system. Women are also more likely to follow through and are 31 percent more effective than men at advancing legislation.[8] In 2013, when the government was on the verge of shutting down, women senators from both parties came together to work out a compromise that both parties could get behind.[9] In fact, the twenty women senators who brokered the deal were widely credited with saving the government from shutdown. Even John McCain (R–AZ) lauded them: "I am very proud that these women are stepping forward. Imagine what they could do if there were fifty of them."[10] Indeed, imagine if the leader of the free world were one of them.

Secondly, women tend to have different policy priorities and put a greater focus on issues that help families, women, and children.[11] Again, it is not just being born a woman that makes women act differently as leaders, but the personal experiences that they bring to their work. As North Dakota Democratic Senator Heidi Heitkamp says of working with her women colleagues: "It is about getting people in a room with different life experiences who will look at things a little differently because they're moms, because they're daughters who've been taking care of senior moms, because they have a different life experience than a lot of senior guys in the room."[12] This means that the needs of everyday American families—better wages, affordable healthcare, and improved school systems for our children—are more likely to be elevated when more women are in charge.

Hillary's election to the presidency will be a game-changer, not only because of the symbolic aspects of her election, but because of the resounding effects it will have on women's representation across the country. American families and our country will be stronger with more women in elected office.

# 3 ➤ She Will Create Jobs and Rebuild Our Infrastructure

*"It's about building our future—a future where the United States will once again lead the world by constructing state-of-the-art infrastructure, creating new jobs and new markets, accelerating the transition to a clean energy economy, and improving the health, safety, and security of all Americans."*

—Hillary Clinton[1]

Rebuilding our nation's infrastructure is part of Hillary's plan to create a strong economy and invest in America's future. Our roads, bridges, and rails are essential to making our economy productive and competitive, but so much of America's infrastructure has deteriorated as government funding in it has declined. Hillary has put forth an ambitious proposal that calls for $275 billion in funding over the next five years to begin to rebuild our nation's infrastructure, create jobs for millions of Americans, and ensure a healthy economy for the future.

Hillary has recognized the importance of investing in infrastructure throughout her career, including in New York after 9/11. Hillary fought to secure $21 billion in federal aid for cleanup and rebuilding in downtown Manhattan, which also helped create thousands of jobs for people in New York City and surrounding areas.[2] Also during her time in the Senate, Hillary fought for several pieces of legislation that would allocate funds toward improving infrastructure, including upgrading roads and highways and expanding public transportation.[3]

As president, Hillary will push a series of plans to invest in building, repairing, and maintaining public infrastructure as part of her overall agenda to create a prosperous future for America. Her plan, which would be fully paid for through business tax reforms, will make smart, targeted investments to improve America's roads and bridges and expand public transportation options.[4] She will also ensure that all Americans can connect to the digital economy with internet access. Hillary believes that high-speed internet access is not a luxury, but a necessity in today's economy. Hillary has a plan to ensure that by 2020, 100 percent of American households will have access to affordable internet services.[5]

Recently, the water crisis in Flint, Michigan, illuminated the need to replace deteriorating pipes and water systems that endanger the health of Americans.[6] Hillary has pushed for funding to deal with the crisis in Flint and fix the water infrastructure.[7] As president, Hillary will prevent catastrophes like Flint from happening in the first place by ensuring systems are updated and modernized, and that no community is left behind.

Hillary's plan to rebuild America's infrastructure will also create millions of good-paying jobs for Americans. The White House Council of Economic Advisers estimates that every $1 billion invested will create 13,000 jobs, meaning that Hillary's five-year plan would produce more than 3.5 million jobs. And these jobs are good ones— the vast majority would pay above the national median wage.[8] Creating good jobs for working Americans is part of Hillary's plan to help American families get ahead and stay ahead.

Updating America's infrastructure will build a twenty-first-century backbone for a twenty-first-century economy. Unlike Republicans who want to reduce investments in infrastructure,[9] Hillary knows that infrastructure is a critical issue that requires a bold, national solution. Hillary's plan signifies an investment in tomorrow that we must make today for America's economy and American families.

# 4 ► She Will Strengthen Our Communities

*"We need to strengthen families and communities because that's where it all starts."*

—Hillary Clinton[1]

Hillary believes that every child—no matter where in America they are born or who their family is—should have the same opportunity to develop their talents and reach their potential. But too many families and communities feel like they've been left behind, and that America's basic bargain—that if you work hard you can get ahead—isn't available to them. That's why as president, Hillary will prioritize an economic agenda that strengthens disadvantaged communities so that all Americans have a fair shot at achieving their dreams.

A strong community is one in which all members have access to good-paying jobs that allow them to take care of themselves and their families. Hillary has spent her career fighting for good wages and job opportunities for Americans. As a senator, Hillary championed legislation to raise the minimum wage[2] and guarantee equal pay for women.[3] She was also a leader in the fight to extend emergency unemployment benefits to families who needed them.[4]

Hillary has spent her career tearing down barriers that hold people back from developing their talents and living up to their potential, especially in communities of color. Part of this work has involved reforming criminal justice systems that are stacked against African Americans. In the Senate, Hillary stood up against racial profiling and was an original co-sponsor of the End Racial Profiling Acts of 2001 and 2004.[5] She has also supported alternatives to mandatory sentencing, like drug treatment programs instead of incarceration, as well as "second chance" programs designed to keep young African Americans out of the criminal justice system.[6]

As president, Hillary will continue her life's work of shattering barriers that hold people back, and will build ladders of opportunity so that Americans everywhere can lift themselves up. At the core of Hillary's policy proposals is equal opportunity: An African American child should have the same chance as a white child, our cities should do as well as our suburbs, and we don't have a single person's talents to waste in building America's future. That's why Hillary has proposed a $50 billion investment to improve infrastructure and create good-paying jobs in the process. In too many communities, people are trapped in poverty because of a lack of opportunities and a crumbling public transportation system. Hillary's plan will revitalize these communities and put people back to work.[7]

Hillary also has specific plans to address issues plaguing communities of color. Her education proposal includes plans to expand opportunities for African Americans by providing assistance to historically black colleges and universities, and incentivizing them to fund the education of students from lower income families.[8] She will also continue her work toward reforming the criminal justice system and strengthening relationships between communities and police forces. Hillary has a plan to train police officers to work in partnership with communities to prevent violent crimes, thereby improving the relations between African American communities and the police officers who serve them.[9]

Finally, Hillary will ensure that the immigrant families who work in and contribute to their communities can stay together. She has pledged not to deport children or families already in the United States who do not have a criminal record.[10] Hillary also supports a roadmap to citizenship[11] and believes in the principle that it is not what you look like or where you come from, but what you contribute to your community and to your country that makes you an American.

Hillary believes that strong communities are the backbone of a strong country, and she will continue her decades-long work to make sure that no American is left behind. Our country needs a leader who can make bold commitments to improving the lives and prospects of American families, and deliver on them, and that leader is Hillary.

# 5 ▶ She Will Protect the Environment for Future Generations

*"We do not have to choose between a healthy environment and a healthy economy."*

—Hillary Clinton[1]

Hillary believes that protecting and preserving our environment and the natural resources it produces are essential to building a brighter future for the next generation. Responsible policies that utilize technological advances and innovation will not only ensure a healthy planet for generations to come, but will also reduce energy costs and produce jobs in the here and now. Clean air and clean water are basic human rights, along with a safe food supply and healthy communities in which to raise our families. Climate change is already having harmful effects on our world, and those effects will be devastating for the next generation if we don't do something about it now. Hillary will take on climate change and promote common sense policies that will encourage a sustainable environment for the next generation, as well as reduce energy costs and create more job opportunities today.

Hillary has been a champion of the environment throughout her career. As senator, Hillary co-sponsored numerous bipartisan initiatives to reduce carbon emissions that contribute to climate change, including the Climate Stewardship and Innovation Act and the Global Warming Pollution Reduction Act.[2] As secretary of state, she strongly supported President Obama's passing of the Clean Power Act, which set the first-ever federal limits on carbon pollution from existing power plants, which cause the most dangerous effects of climate change.[3] Hillary also brought together representatives from thirty-seven countries and forty-four NGOs to form the Climate and Clean Air Coalition, a group dedicated to advocating for common sense solutions to reduce methane and other harmful pollutants in the environment.[4]

As president, Hillary will prioritize addressing environmental concerns and ensuring that the next generation inherits a healthy, sustainable environment. She considers the deleterious effects of climate change to be "the most consequential, urgent, sweeping collection of challenges we face as a nation and a world,"[5] and her policy proposals are aimed at finding solutions to these challenges. And while the issue is global in scope, Hillary wants to start the work right here at home, and exert American leadership on these issues.

Hilary will continue her unwavering support of President Obama's power plant regulations and as president, she will defend them from attack.[6] She will incentivize the development and use of clean energy and will invest in the modernization of the country's infrastructure, including repairing or replacing oil and gas pipelines that are outdated and risk both oil and methane leaks and other hazardous accidents that could devastate the environment.[7] Hillary's goal is to make America a clean energy superpower in the world. She is ambitious in her goals, and her plans include a 700 percent increase in the country's solar capacity by 2020, the equivalent of 25 million fully operational rooftop systems.[8]

Because Hillary is committed to ensuring that every American has the opportunity to get ahead, she pays special attention to the environmental concerns of disadvantaged populations, including families living in low-income neighborhoods. For example, she stood up for the people of Flint, Michigan, who, for two years, had been drinking water contaminated with lead, and demanded that the governor put funds toward the long-term health needs of children with lead poisoning.[9] Hillary's support for the people of Flint reflects her unwavering commitment to ensuring that Americans everywhere can live and work in a healthy, safe environment. As she said: "We know there are more Flints out there, many places where low-income communities and communities of color are struggling to deal with lead paint, toxic soil, unsafe water and air, and I'm just not going to accept the status quo."[10]

Hillary's vision for a sustainable environment that will benefit Americans today and tomorrow directly contrasts with the GOP's plan to roll back environmental protections and allow corporations to violate the earth. She will ensure that every American, regardless of where they live, can enjoy the benefits of a healthy, safe environment.[11] Hillary represents the future and will ensure that our environmental policies move our country forward.

**She Gets Work/Life Balance**

*"It's outrageous that America is the only country in the developed world that doesn't guarantee paid leave."*

—Hillary Clinton[1]

Hillary knows that when families are strong, countries are strong. But in today's world, Americans are working more hours than ever before, which translates to less time spent with family.[2] This is especially a problem when a family member is sick and needs care or when a parent welcomes a new baby into their family. Nearly 90 percent of American workers do not have any paid family leave,[3] and more than 43 million Americans, over half of whom are working mothers, don't have a single paid sick day.[4,5]

As First Lady, Hillary campaigned hard for the Family and Medical Leave Act (FMLA), which was passed under her husband's administration.[6] But while FMLA was a start, it is limited in its reach and effectiveness since it only guarantees unpaid leave. For many, that's no guarantee at all. Hillary believes that having to choose between being there for family and putting food on the table is a choice no one should have to make. She knows that times have changed and we finally need to update our workplace laws to catch up with the realities of working families' lives.

Throughout her career, Hillary has been a staunch advocate for policies and rules that allow families to balance work outside of the home with their personal lives. In the Senate, she repeatedly co-sponsored and pushed for legislation that would guarantee paid sick and family leave,[7] arguing that not only are policies that respect the work/life balance good for families, they also benefit our economy.[8] Numerous studies have shown that paid leave boosts family economic security, worker productivity, the supply of labor, and overall economic growth.[9] Americans overwhelmingly favor these policies—a 2015 national poll found that nearly 90 percent of Americans support ensuring all workers earn paid sick days to care for themselves or family members, and majority support holds across party lines.[10]

Republicans like Ted Cruz want to let employers deny their employees paid family leave, even in the face of studies that show these policies actually help grow the economy. Hillary believes that we need common sense policies that support working families, because being there when your family needs you shouldn't be negotiable, and as president, Hillary will ensure that no American worker will have to choose between their family and a paycheck. The world has changed, and Hillary will ensure our workplace rules are fair and make life work for American families.

# 7 ➤ She Will Advocate for Millennials

*"As I speak with young people across the country in Iowa, New Hampshire, and elsewhere, I do sense this real feeling of being somehow disadvantaged, put on the wrong side of American opportunity. And I understand that . . . I'm going to do everything I can to reach out and to explain why good ideas on paper are important. But you've got to be able to translate them into action to get results for people. I have a lot [of] experience doing that. I think I can deliver positive change for young people in our country."*

—Hillary Clinton[1]

Hillary knows that millennials are vital to America's future and wants to ensure that every millennial can get ahead and stay ahead. That's why she is committed to addressing the issues that young people face today and ensuring their voices are heard. What many millennials don't know is that Hillary not only has a record of fighting for the interests of young people, but she has plans to address key issues, like college affordability and student loans, that will help ensure that every young American has the opportunity to live up to their potential.

Hillary has fought to make college more affordable throughout her career. "The burden of student loan debt can put people in economic handcuffs,"[2] Hillary said when she introduced several pieces of legislation in the Senate aimed at helping students repay their loans.[3] She also pushed for legislation that would ensure lenders make the borrowing process more transparent to students, so that they can make educated, informed decisions about their loans.[4] Hillary also worked on efforts to make education more accessible and affordable for returning veterans.[5]

Today, Americans hold $1.2 trillion in student debt and more than 8 million students have had to default on their loans.[5] Hillary believes these statistics are unacceptable and has a plan to address them. Called the "New College Compact," Hillary's strategy involves a series of bold proposals that will significantly reduce the cost of higher education and avoid crippling student debt.[7] Under the Compact, states will be incentivized to drastically lower their tuition fees so that students do not have to take out loans at four-year public colleges and universities, and tuition at community colleges will be free.[8] The plan will also allow students to refinance their current loans at lower rates, which will help alleviate the burdens on 25 million individuals.[9] Hillary will also extend the American Opportunity Tax Credit, which allows families to save up to $2,500 per student to help with college tuition and other educational costs.[10] The beauty of Hillary's plan is that she intends to pay for it by closing tax loopholes and making the wealthy pay their fair share.[11]

In addition to ensuring that costs are not a barrier to young people accessing higher education, Hillary is also deeply committed to many of the social issues that young people care about. For example, Hillary has been a champion of women's reproductive health for decades. As Cecile Richards, President of Planned Parenthood, noted in her endorsement of Hillary in the primary: "No other candidate in our nation's history has demonstrated such a strong commitment to women or such a clear record on behalf of women's health and rights."[12] As president, Hillary will continue to stand up for Planned Parenthood and a woman's right to make her own reproductive health choices. She will also make contraception more affordable and available to women and will prevent insurance companies from discriminating against covering women because of their reproductive health needs.[13]

Hillary also supports the LGBT community and has outlined a plan that would ensure LGBT rights and protections are extended across society. In July 2015, she announced her support for the Equality Act of 2015, which expands the 1964 Civil Rights Act to include comprehensive protection for LGBT individuals in the areas of credit, education, employment, housing, federal financial assistance, jury service and public accommodations.[14] Many consider the Equality Act the next big fight for LGBT rights,[15] and Hillary is prepared to take this fight on and win so that all Americans can live their lives free from discrimination. Her position is radically different from the stance of the Republicans who want to roll back the great progress our country has made on this front.

In addition to addressing the issues millennials face today, Hillary will also look forward, to the issues millennials will confront tomorrow. One of those issues is the caregiving crisis, which millennials will begin to face in coming years as their parents grow older. Hillary has proposed providing a tax credit of up to $6,000 per family to help offset the costs of caring for elderly relatives.[16] And over the next 10 years, Hillary will invest $100 million in new initiatives to help address the soaring costs of caregiving and help alleviate the financial pressure that many millennials will face.[17]

This campaign has critical importance for the direction of our country, and the election of Hillary Clinton will ensure our country moves forward, and that no American is left behind. Hillary will fight for millennials and the issues they care about, because she knows how important this generation is to America's future.

# 8 ⟩ She Will Make Child Care a Priority

*"When we talk about child care, we're talking about the economy, we're talking about families, we're talking about fairness. We're talking about all the values that we believe are necessary to raise healthy, successful, productive children in society today."*
—Hillary Clinton[1]

Hillary believes that in today's economy, when having both parents in the workforce is an economic necessity, providing access to affordable, quality child care should be a national priority. Too many American families struggle to balance work and family, with some even dropping out of the workforce altogether because of the dearth of child care options.[2] This prevents American families from getting ahead and staying ahead. Hillary's plan to ensure every American family has access to affordable, quality child care is not a luxury, but a growth strategy that will boost America's economy. To Hillary, these are not just family issues, but economic issues that affect all of our country, because policies that strengthen families strengthen America.

Hillary has always been a champion for families, women, and children, and her record on child care reflects that. In the Senate, she fought continuously for legislation that would expand child care funding and give American families access to affordable care.[3] She also reached across the aisle to work with Republican Senator John Thune (SD) on legislation that would allow children whose parents have died while in service to our nation to retain their federal child care benefits.[4]

Hillary knows that access to child care is only one piece of a larger effort to provide a strong foundation for American families. She believes that equal pay, paid family leave, and living wages are also critical policies that are needed in order to ensure economic growth in our country. She has been a passionate supporter of these issues throughout her career. In the Senate, she championed the

Paycheck Fairness Act and co-sponsored the Lilly Ledbetter Fair Pay Act in an effort to ensure equal pay and help close the wage gap.[5] She fought for legislation to guarantee paid sick leave and paid parental leave for all federal employees, so that Americans don't have to choose between a paycheck and being there for their family.[6]

As president, Hillary will incorporate access to affordable, quality child care into her overall plan to strengthen and grow America's economy and ensure American workers are able to take care of their families and make a decent living at the same time. She has proposed expanding on-campus child care options for college students who are parents, thereby ensuring that parents are able to meet their family responsibilities while also getting an education that will help them get ahead.[7] She will also build on the great work that the Obama Administration has begun to expand access to child care, including tax cuts to help families cope with rising child care costs. She will expand Early Head Start, a federally funded program that provides education and health services to low-income families with young children.[8]

Hillary's commitment to investing in child care reflects her vision of ensuring every American family has the opportunity to get ahead and stay ahead. With Hillary in charge, "middle class" will mean something again, and "economic mobility" will no longer sound like a lofty relic of the past, but will be a reality for the future of America.

# 9 ▶ She Will Invest in Our Children

*"When I look at my new granddaughter, I think to myself, we are going to do everything we can to make sure she has opportunities in life. But what about all the kids? You should not have to be the grandchild of a former president to know that you can make it in America."*

—Hillary Clinton[1]

Hillary's vision for America's future involves breaking down barriers and building ladders so that every child in America has a fair shot. In America, hard work and perseverance should be rewarded, but too often it is the family you are born into, or the community that you grow up in, that predict your future chances for success. Hillary wants to change that and restore the basic bargain that if you work hard, you can get ahead. That starts with ensuring that every child can get a good start in life, no matter where they come from.

Hillary has focused on the needs of children throughout her career, and credits her own mother as her inspiration. Hillary's mother, Dorothy, was abandoned as a child and had to go to work at a young age to support herself. As Hillary explains it: "Learning about my mother's childhood sparked my strong conviction that every child deserves a chance to live up to her God-given potential and that we should never quit on any child."[2]

Right after law school, when most of Hillary's peers were taking jobs at top-paying law firms, Hillary joined the Children's Defense Fund, an advocacy group that fights for the rights and interests of children. One of her first projects with the CDF was going door-to-door to collect information and compile data on children who either dropped out of school or were falling behind due to physical, mental, or learning disabilities. She used this data to craft a landmark report by the CDF that helped raise awareness of the plight of handicapped children and eventually led to the passage of the Americans with Disabilities Act.[3]

As First Lady, Hillary worked with members of the Senate to craft and build support for the State Children's Health Insurance Program (CHIP) which provides increased healthcare coverage for children in low-income families.[4] CHIP was a tremendous success: 15 years after it was launched, the number of uninsured children was halved from 14 to 7 percent, providing coverage to more than 8 million children.[5]

Part of Hillary's plan to move America forward involves ensuring that the children of today have a fair shot in life. She has proposed doubling the funding for Early Head Start and related child care programs[6] and has called for universal preschool education for every child in America. Her proposal would guarantee that in the next ten years, every four year old in America has access to high-quality preschool.[7] Hillary believes that getting off to a good start is every child's birthright, and she will see to it that our country funds and supports programs that give children opportunities for success.

Much evidence points to the long-term benefits of high-quality early childhood education programs that Hillary supports. A study by the White House Council of Economic Advisers found that greater investments in early learning will translate to societal benefits of $8.60 for every $1 spent initially, half of which comes from increased earnings for children once they are adults.[8] But despite the overwhelming evidence of benefits, Republicans want to cut funding for early childhood education, and some want to eliminate existing programs altogether.[9] Hillary will support America's children and work to ensure that every child—no matter where they are born or to whom they are born—has a fair shot at success in this country.

# 10 ▶ She Is Committed to Supporting Our Youth

*"Prediction from a grown-up: Your future is going to be amazing. You will surprise yourself with what you're capable of and the incredible things you go on to do. Find the people who love and believe in you— there will be lots of them."*

—Hillary Clinton, commenting on a photo of a struggling gay teen that was posted on *Humans of New York*[1]

Hillary believes that every young American should have the opportunities they need to develop their talents. But many youth in America live in communities where jobs are scarce, education is failing, and infrastructure is crumbling. Hillary wants to make sure that every young person has a fair shot in life, and she will knock down the barriers to establish pathways to opportunity for every child.

Hillary believes that every child, no matter his or her background, should be guaranteed a high-quality education. That is why she has worked her entire career to improve public school systems around the country, and particularly in disadvantaged communities that need a helping hand. As First Lady of Arkansas, she led the fight to raise academic standards as the chair of the Arkansas Educational Standards Commission.[2] As First Lady of the United States, she chaired the first-ever conference devoted to improving educational opportunities for Latino youth.[3] In the Senate, Hillary served on the Health, Education, and Labor Committee where she fought to improve educational opportunities for the country's most disadvantaged students.[4] Hillary's lifelong commitment to lifting up schools and supporting teachers in public school systems led to the National Education Association's endorsement of her in the 2016 primary.[5]

As president, Hillary will expand on her work to improve public schools and will make access to high-quality education a priority of her administration. She will work to support the effective implementation of the Every Student Succeeds Act, legislation signed by President Obama that gives states and teachers flexibility to address the needs of their students while also holding schools accountable for the achievement of all children, particularly low-income students, students of color, and students with disabilities. Hillary will also make investments in early learning programs, so that every child can get a good start and every student has a fair shot at the education they need to be prepared for the twenty-first-century workforce.[6]

In addition to continuing her important work on K through 12 education, Hillary will also support America's youth by reducing unemployment. About 1 in 10 youth between the ages of 16 and 24 are unemployed, which is more than twice the national average.[7] Hillary will put young people to work by incentivizing businesses to establish apprenticeship programs, investing $20 billion to create jobs in local communities, and supporting entrepreneurship and small business growth in underserved communities with federal grants.[8] Hillary believes that the youth of America in every zip code deserve a chance to put their talents to use and have every opportunity to get ahead in life.

As president, Hillary will continue her lifelong work of supporting America's youth and will make the necessary investments to build up the pipeline of opportunity. This is a very different strategy from the Republicans who have a history of trying to slash funding for education[9] and are more interested in catering to wealthy special interests than addressing the issues facing the youth of America. Under Hillary's leadership, no youth will be left behind, as she will ensure we make the necessary investment to provide opportunities to America's next generation.

# 11 ► She Will Expand Space Exploration

*"I would like to see us continue to explore space. There's just a lot for us to keep learning. I think it's a good investment . . . we're at the brink of all kinds of new information. Let's not back off now."*

—Hillary Clinton [1]

Space exploration is critical to scientific knowledge and advancement. So far, human beings have explored only a fraction of the vast universe of planets and stars, and there is much more to discover. Hillary wants America to take the lead in pursuing scientific advancement and discovery of outer space. Supporting space exploration is part of Hillary's vision to bring America forward into the future, and to establish our country as a leader in the twenty-first century.

Hillary has been fascinated with outer space since she was a child. When she was 14, she wrote to NASA to ask how she could become an astronaut. NASA responded that they did not accept women astronauts.[2] Nevertheless, Hillary's passion for space exploration never waned, and as a US senator she supported the Vision for Space Exploration, a 2005 NASA authorization bill, which would send human astronauts to the moon and eventually to Mars.[3]

As president, Hillary will renew America's commitment to space exploration programs, a commitment weakened in recent years as some elected officials have tried to cut funding for NASA.[4] She will ensure that NASA has the funding it needs to go further than they have gone before and continue to make valuable discoveries that contribute to our scientific knowledge and development.[5] Hillary will also ensure the earth is protected from outer space threats and will invest more money in tracking and monitoring asteroids, in order to protect human civilization from a deadly impact.[6]

With Republicans in Congress looking to cut spending wherever it can be found, America needs a leader who can stand up for science. Human beings have made some incredible discoveries in space recently, including the New Horizons mission to Pluto[7] and the discovery of water on Mars.[8] These findings are incredibly valuable in understanding our place in the universe and give us tremendous insight into the future of our own planet. America needs a president who doesn't view NASA as an acceptable sacrifice, but as necessary for advancing our scientific capabilities and leadership in the twenty-first century.

# 12 ▶ She Will Make Renewable Energy Mainstream

*"We're on the cusp of a new era. We can have more choice in the energy we consume and produce. We can create a more open, efficient, and resilient grid that connects us, empowers us, improves our health, and benefits us all."*

—Hillary Clinton[1]

Hillary believes climate change is an urgent threat that America must address now. The world's reliance on fossil fuels is the primary reason why the earth is getting warmer and warmer,[2] and we will continue to see rising sea levels, unprecedented heat waves, and tropical storms.[3] In order to ensure the sustainability of our planet and prevent the catastrophic consequences of failing to act, we need to transition to renewable energy sources. Hillary has a plan that will make renewable energy mainstream in America, and in the process create millions of jobs and elevate America as the world's clean energy superpower.

Throughout her career, Hillary has fought for clean energy and pushed to reduce reliance on fossil fuels. As senator, Hillary supported the Clean Power Act to reduce toxic air pollutants, including greenhouse gases.[4] She also supported legislation that increased subsidies for renewable energy exploration, and eliminated subsidies for oil and gas companies.[5] She was instrumental as secretary of state in securing the 2009 Copenhagen Accord, a landmark international agreement, in which the United States and other major producers of greenhouse gasses such as China, India, and Brazil committed to mutual reductions in greenhouse gas emissions.[6]

As president, Hillary will go further than any president has ever gone before when it comes to clean energy. Her bold, ambitious plan to make renewable energy mainstream includes two goals:

1. The United States will generate enough renewable energy to power every home in the country within 10 years of Hillary taking office.[7]

2. The United States will have more than half a billion solar panels installed across the country by the end of Hillary's first term in office.[8]

The crux of Hillary's energy strategy promotes active partnerships between federal, state, and local officials to incentivize renewable energy use and investment through tax credits as well as the repeal of unnecessary regulations.[9] In addition to her proactive strategy of encouraging renewable energy, Hillary will also defend our country against the fossil fuel industry's attacks on federal energy standards, pollution regulation, and other initiatives to make clean energy the future of this country.

Republicans aren't committed to renewable energy because so many Republicans continue to deny the science of climate change.[10] While it won't be easy to make renewable energy mainstream, Hillary is up to the challenge and understands how critical it is to act today, not tomorrow. As she said recently: "I am just a grandmother with two eyes and a brain and I know what is happening in the world is going to have a big effect on my daughter and especially my granddaughters. You don't have to be a scientist to take on this urgent challenge that threatens us all. You just have to be willing to act."[11]

And willing to act she is. Serious investment in renewable energy will reduce America's contribution to climate change, and will exemplify American leadership on this critical issue. Hillary Clinton's energy policies will put Americans to work, significantly reduce carbon emissions, and contribute to a more sustainable world.

# 13 ▶ She Believes in the American Dream

*"It's America's basic bargain. If you do your part you ought to be able to get ahead. And when everybody does their part, America gets ahead too."*

—Hillary Clinton[1]

Hillary believes that every American should have an equal opportunity to build a good life for themselves and their families. Hard work should be rewarded, and everyone should have an equal shot at being a part of the middle class. But this basic bargain that in many ways defines America seems increasingly elusive. Since 2000, worker productivity has increased by 25 percent, yet wages have remained stagnant for everyone but the top 1 percent of earners.[2] Four out of ten children born to the lowest income families never make it out of poverty.[3] A majority of African American children, whose families fought their way into the middle class decades ago, now have lower incomes than their parents did, and many are falling out of the middle class altogether.[4] And women continue to be paid less money for the same work that men do.[5] Hillary wants to change these alarming statistics so that every American has the opportunity to live up to their potential, and the American Dream is restored.

Hillary has advocated for equal opportunity for all Americans throughout her career. As senator, she fought for higher, fairer wages for working Americans, voting to increase the minimum wage[6] and for equal pay for women.[7] She also supported progressive tax policies that included tax cuts for the middle class and made the wealthiest pay their fair share. Hillary also pushed for early childhood education for children from low-income families.[8] Her commitment to increasing opportunities for all Americans is reflective of Hillary's vision for an America where everyone can share in prosperity and what this great country has to offer—not just billionaires and corporations.

Hillary has outlined several proposals that are part of her plan to help hardworking American families get ahead and stay ahead. Her plan to make college more affordable will invest $350 billion so that students do not have to burden themselves with loans to pay tuition at public universities in their states.[9] Hillary will also reduce the interest on student loans, saving more than 25 million Americans about $2,000 on their loan repayments.[10] She will also implement a tax cut of $2,500 per college student to help pay for education. Hillary believes that any American who is willing to work hard and wants to better themselves by obtaining a college degree should be able to do so without drowning in debt.

She has also put forth several initiatives to build a strong, fair economy that will work for American families. Hillary knows that despite working longer hours than ever before, American families do not have the income they need to deal with the rising costs of healthcare, child care, and education. Hillary believes that raising incomes for hardworking Americans is the defining economic challenge of our time, and she will raise the minimum wage for American workers to $12 an hour.[11] She will also fight for equal pay for women, which is not just a women's issue, but an economic issue that will benefit all Americans. Her plan also incentivizes companies who share their profits with the employees who make them, so that more working Americans can share in the rewards of success.[12]

Republicans want to cut taxes for the wealthy and allow corporations to play by their own rules instead of creating more opportunities for hardworking Americans to make it to the middle class. Their America is one where only a select few can share in the American Dream, where the playing field is unequal, and where the deck is stacked against working Americans.[13] Hillary's America is the America of the future—a country that honors the basic bargain that no matter who you are or where you come from, if you work hard and play by the rules, you'll have the opportunity to build a good life for yourself and your family.

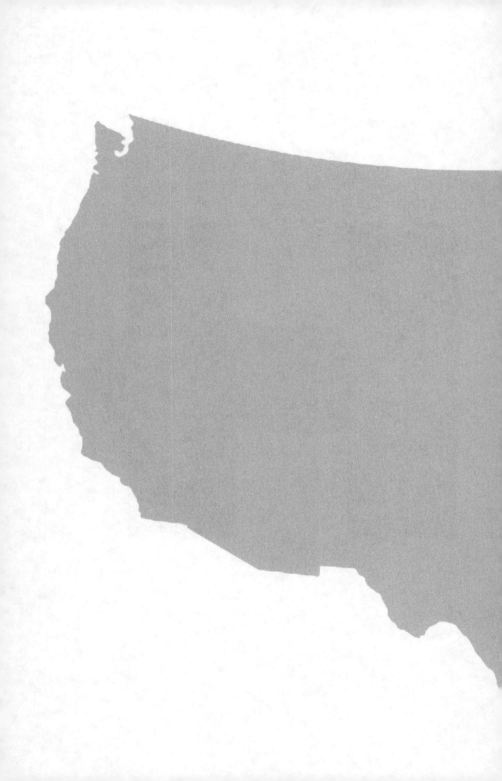

# II

## Fairness

# 14 ▶ She Will Create a Strong and Fair Economy for All Americans

*"I want to see our economy work for the struggling, the striving and the successful."*

—Hillary Clinton[1]

Hillary believes that raising incomes for hardworking American families is the economic challenge of our time. For the past forty years, Americans have worked harder and longer while wages have stagnated.[2] This means that although Americans are working more productively than ever, the fruits of their labors have primarily benefitted those at the top.[3] Hillary believes we need to create a fair economy that allows hardworking families to get ahead and stay ahead, so that their economic future is secure, and so that children of the next generation can inherit an economy that allows them to thrive.

Hillary has a lifetime of experience fighting for economic policies that benefit middle-class families. Twenty years ago as First Lady, she successfully advocated for increasing the minimum wage, recognizing that Americans simply could not raise a family on $4.25 an hour, and that supporting families is fundamental to creating strong, healthy communities.[4] For the same reasons, she voted to raise the minimum wage as senator, and repeatedly introduced legislation tying increases in the salaries of members of Congress with increases in the federal minimum wage for working families.[5]

Hillary believes economic growth should be strong, fair, and long-term, and her plan to raise incomes for American families and grow the economy are centered on these three fundamental principles.[6] She will strengthen our economy by investing in infrastructure and clean energy, which will create millions of jobs. Hillary is also calling for tax relief for American families, including extending a $2,500 tax cut for students and cutting taxes for businesses that share profits with their employees.[7] Finally, Hillary knows that small businesses are the backbone of a strong economy, which is why her plan supports small business growth by expanding access to capital, providing tax relief, cutting red tape,[8] and helping small businesses bring their goods to new markets.[9]

Creating a strong and fair economy isn't possible when the deck is stacked against hardworking American families. Hillary will reform the tax code so that corporations and the wealthiest have to pay their fair share of taxes. She supports the Buffett Rule that ensures no millionaire pays a lower tax rate than his or her secretary.[10] Her plan also calls for corporations to share more of their profits with workers, rather than concentrating the wealth at the top.[11] She will also fight for equal pay for women, paid family leave, and affordable child care—policies that are not only fair, but part of a growth strategy for our economy.

Hillary understands that a strong and fair economy means raising the federal minimum wage to $12 an hour, a wage that will allow over 35 million American workers and their families[12] a fair shot at success and a path toward a secure economic future.[13] Raising the minimum wage would have profound effects on all American workers, but in particular women, workers of color, and single parents. And a higher wage will not only benefit American workers, but will also have a stimulative effect on the economy.[14]

Planning for a strong and fair economy over the long term means not only finding ways to grow families' incomes, but also to protect their economic security from financial crises that hurt our economy and set our country back. The George W. Bush administration let Wall Street write its own rules, and the cost to Americans has been devastating—9 million workers lost their jobs, 5 million families lost their homes, and more than $13 trillion in household wealth was wiped out.[15] Hillary's plan holds Wall Street accountable so that middle-class families never have to bail out Wall Street again. She will defend the protections that were put in place after the Great Recession, and will go further to tackle dangerous risks in the financial system and hold both individuals and corporations accountable when they break the law or put the system at risk.[16] Her plan will uphold the basic principles of fairness and promote economic security for American families.

Hillary has also strongly opposed plans espoused by Republicans, including those guided by the "trickle-down economics" theory, which have failed repeatedly.[17] As Hillary herself explains, "There is a pattern of Republicans getting us into economic messes, and Democratic presidents having to come in and clean them up."[18] With Republicans in charge, Wall Street would go unrestricted, wealth would remain concentrated at the top while American workers struggle to get by, and policies would benefit big corporations over small businesses.[19]

The next administration will have a profound effect on our country's economic security and the future of our next generation. The choice is clear—while the Republicans want to return to failed economic policies that benefit the wealthy and corporations, Hillary's plan moves our country forward and creates a strong, fair economy that works for all Americans over the long term. She will build the economy of tomorrow, today.

# 15 ▶ She Will Strengthen Our Democracy

*"I believe every citizen has the right to vote. And I believe we should do everything we can to make it easier for every citizen to vote . . . Yes, this is about democracy. But it's also about dignity. About the ability to stand up and say, yes, I am a citizen. I am an American. My voice counts."*

—Hillary Clinton[1]

Hillary believes our political system should be free, fair, and accessible, and that every eligible American who wants to do their civic duty and vote should have the opportunity to have their voice heard. Not only is voting a fundamental bedrock of American democracy, but it is essential to ensuring that the voices of all Americans are reflected in public policy.

Hillary has a long history of advocating for policies that increase opportunities for eligible citizens to participate in our democracy. In 1993, she was an ardent supporter of the National Voter Registration Act (NVRA), a law that increased opportunities for voter registration to occur at the same time as other transactions, like applying for a driver's license at the DMV, or veterans' benefits at the VA. The NVRA has significantly reduced the costs associated with registering to vote, eliminated errors on the voters rolls, and has given tens of millions of Americans the opportunity to have their voices heard.[2]

Recently, Hillary has proposed bold federal legislation that would modernize voter registration and bring our system into the twenty-first century. Under her plan, citizens would automatically be registered to vote on their eighteenth birthdays, unless they chose to opt-out. Hillary's program will enable state election boards to streamline their rolls, so that they can keep them up to date in case an individual moves to a different district or state. This eliminates errors on the rolls, keeps them current, and ensures eligible voters who want to vote are not turned away at the polls. She has also called for increased opportunities for early voting, including on weekends, so that working Americans can have a voice.[3]

Hillary also opposes restrictive laws, like requiring registered voters to provide specific types of photo ID that millions of people don't have, slashing the number of available polling stations, and eliminating early voting. She wants to stop Republicans from turning back the clock on voting rights by passing restrictive voting laws for their own political gain, so they can control who votes for them in the next election. These policies make it harder for eligible Americans to vote, including people of color, disabled Americans, and young people, who are less likely to have the necessary form of ID.[4] Voter ID laws also place burdens on seniors—who often don't have their birth certificates and can't get the proper ID—as well as service members and veterans who are constantly moving and may not meet the strict residency requirements.[5]

Protecting the integrity of our election system is important, but we must be careful not to undermine free and fair access to the ballot in the name of preventing voter fraud. And study after study has shown that actual occurrences of voter fraud are almost nonexistent.[6] But Republicans cling to the myth of voter fraud in order to stoke voters' fears and convince them that restrictive photo ID laws that disenfranchise millions of people, including seniors and veterans, will protect our elections. As Hillary said of her Republican opponents: "They should stop fear-mongering about a phantom epidemic of election fraud and start explaining why they're so scared of letting citizens have their say. What part of democracy are they afraid of?"[7]

Hillary will strengthen our democracy and increase opportunities for citizen participation to ensure that the voices of everyday Americans are reflected in public policy. In contrast to the Republicans, she wants to move voting rights forward, not backward. It's time the voters take back our government and make our democracy of, by, and for the people.

# 16 ▶ She Will Tackle Economic Inequality

*"We need to have people believing that their work will be rewarded. So I'm going to do everything I can to try to get that deck reshuffled so being middle class means something again."*

—Hillary Clinton[1]

Economic inequality in America has reached unprecedented levels. The *top one-tenth of 1 percent* in this country possess nearly the same share of wealth as the bottom 90 percent of Americans.[2] Over the past 30 years, the top 1 percent of earners have seen their incomes increase by over 256 percent; in contrast, the bottom 90 percent have barely seen their paychecks budge.[3] Yet Americans have been working harder than ever before: in the past 15 years, productivity has increased by 22 percent while wages have increased by just 2 percent.[4] The deck is stacked against American families and in favor of corporations who enjoy near-record profits because they were able to rig the rules of the economy in their favor. Hillary believes tackling economic inequality is among the most critical issues of our day, and that large-scale changes are needed in order to restore America's basic bargain that if you work hard, you can get ahead in life.

Hillary has a long history of fighting against economic inequality and for American families. She has always been a strong supporter of raising the minimum wage, and as a senator she authored the 2006 and 2007 versions of the Standing With Minimum Wage Earners Act, which proposed tying Congressional salary increases with minimum wage increases for working families.[5] Hillary has also been a champion of equal pay for women, and introduced two versions of the Paycheck Fairness Act to prevent employer retaliation against workers who inquire about their wages, and also give women the tools they need to negotiate for equal pay.[6]

Throughout her career, Hillary has fought for lower taxes for middle-class families and has pushed for the wealthy and corporations to pay their fair share. In the Senate she opposed the Bush tax cuts for the wealthy[7] as well as GOP proposals to eliminate the estate tax on inherited wealth for the very rich.[8] And at the same time that she opposed Republican tax policies that cater to the wealthy, Hillary also supported numerous tax cuts for the middle class, such as tax credits for student loan recipients.[9]

Hillary has set forth an ambitious proposal to attack economic inequality in America and has made raising middle-class family incomes the heart of her plan. She will raise the federal minimum wage to $12 an hour[10] and also supports states and cities that want to raise their local minimum wages to $15 an hour.[11] She will also make sure American workers are able to benefit from the profits they help create by providing a 15 percent tax credit for companies that share profits with their employees.[12] Finally, she will make sure women receive equal pay for equal work by promoting transparency and holding employers accountable for pay disparities.[13] These are policies that not only help women, but help grow the economy as a whole, so all of America benefits.[14]

Hillary will also make bold changes to the tax code to make it fairer. She supports the Buffett Rule, which ensures that millionaires won't pay a lower tax rate than their secretaries.[15] She will also close the loopholes that allow the super wealthy to pay a lower tax rate than the workers who clean their offices. Making the top 1 percent pay their fair share of taxes would generate $157 billion in revenue in her first year of office alone, which will fund Hillary's education initiatives, including her plan to make college affordable and provide universal pre-K.[16]

Hillary believes that while talent is universal, opportunity is not, and it is the next president's responsibility to create as many opportunities as possible so that all Americans have a fair shot. That's why combating economic inequality and raising incomes for middle-class Americans are among Hillary's top priorities. Hillary's vision is very different from the vision of Republicans like Donald Trump, who have tax plans that disproportionately benefit the top 1 percent.[17] Hillary will bring our country forward, smashing the barriers that have held American families back for too long and creating pathways to help them move up.

 **She Will Fight for Equal Pay**

*"We need to make equal pay and equal opportunity for women and girls a reality so women's rights are human rights for once and for all."*
—Hillary Clinton[1]

Hillary knows that when women are strong, families are strong, and when families are strong, countries are strong. That's why equal pay is a central issue in her campaign. Not only is this issue about fairness, it's about ensuring that our economy can grow and that our country can compete globally. Economic experts agree with Hillary: remedying the pay gap would help stimulate our economy, strengthen the middle class, and attack poverty.[2]

In 2015, women made on average 78 cents to a man's dollar, an unacceptable statistic that embarrasses our country.[3]

While Republicans continue to subscribe to dated notions of family structures and gender roles, Hillary understands that changing times call for updated policies that move our country forward. Gone are the days of men bringing home the bacon while women fry it up in the pan. The world has changed, and our rules need to sprint to catch up. We all work hard and we all—women and men—deserve to be paid equally for equal work.

Hillary has a long history of spearheading legislation on equal pay. In the Senate, she introduced and advocated for the Paycheck Fairness Act, which would take critical steps to empower women to negotiate for equal pay. She co-sponsored the historic Lilly Ledbetter Fair Pay Act, which expanded the rights of women to seek recourse for unequal pay.[4]

She also called out the Bush Administration's failure to enforce equal pay laws. Hillary pushed an investigation which found the administration had not monitored the enforcement of pay equity regulations. More recently, she has blasted GOP figures like Scott Walker who called equal pay a "bogus" issue, Marco Rubio who called the equal pay issue a waste of time, and Donald Trump whose answer to the equal pay issue is to tell women to do a better job.[5] Hillary's response to these outdated, out of touch comments echo what the vast majority of Americans are thinking: "What century are they living in?"[6]

As president, Hillary will continue to fight for equal pay, so that women, families, and our country can thrive. She has outlined a plan that would give women the tools they need to fight workplace discrimination and promote pay transparency across our economy so that women have the information they need to negotiate fairly.[7] The cornerstone of her plan, the Paycheck Fairness Act, holds employers accountable by requiring them to prove that wage discrepancies are tied to legitimate business qualifications and not gender, and by prohibiting companies from taking retaliatory action against employees who raise concerns about gender-based wage discrimination.

Economists have found that if women received pay equal to men, positive effects would reverberate across America's economy. Paying women equally would have added an additional $448 billion (equivalent to almost 3 percent of GDP) to America's economy, about the equivalent of adding another state the size of Virginia to the nation. The poverty rate of working women and their families would fall by half, from 8.1 percent to 3.9 percent. The total increase in women's earnings with equal pay is equivalent to more than 14 times what federal and state governments spent in one year on welfare benefits.[8] Hillary's commitment to ensure equal pay will grow the economy, strengthen families, and bring our country closer to its ideal of fairness and equality for all Americans.

# 18 ▶ She Will Ensure That All Americans Have Access to Healthcare

*"All of the Republican candidates for president are determined to get rid of the Affordable Care Act. I tell you, I am not going to let them rip away the progress we made, I am not going to let them tear up that law, kick 16 million people off health coverage and force this country to start the health care debate all over again. Not on my watch."*
—Hillary Clinton[1]

American families benefit from healthy communities, where everyone has access to affordable, quality healthcare from a provider of their choice, at the time they need it, and at a cost they can afford. Hillary believes that access to affordable healthcare should not be a privilege for the wealthy, but a basic human right of all American citizens. The Affordable Care Act (ACA) was successful in helping millions of Americans access basic care, but there is more work to be done to ensure that the 32 million Americans who are still uninsured[2] can get access to the care they need. Rather than tear the law up, start over, and turn back the clock as Republicans and even some Democrats have suggested, Hillary will build on what is among President Obama's greatest accomplishments and improve the law so that more Americans can exercise their basic human right to healthcare.

Hillary has been a champion of affordable healthcare for decades. As First Lady, she refused to give up when Congress defeated healthcare reform. Instead, she worked across the aisle, with both Republicans and Democrats, to create the Children's Health Insurance Program (CHIP), which now provides health coverage to more than 8 million children.[3]

As a senator, Hillary fought hard to reduce the costs of healthcare for American families and stop insurance companies from rigging the system and charging exorbitant amounts for coverage.[4] And after the terrorist attacks of 9/11, Hillary secured $20 billion from the Bush Administration for recovery and to take care of the first responders who suffered long-term health effects from their valiant efforts at Ground Zero.[5]

As president, Hillary will continue her lifelong work and commitment to ensuring the right to affordable healthcare is realized in America, as it is in every other industrialized democracy.[6] Hillary will build on President Obama's successes and defend the ACA, but also improve the law so that more Americans can afford coverage with the doctor of their choice. One way Hillary will accomplish this is through tax credits of up to $5,000 for families whose out-of-pocket healthcare expenses exceed more than 5 percent of the family's total income.[7] She will also require insurance companies to be more transparent about costs and coverage so that families can make good, well-informed choices about their healthcare.[8] To Hillary, it is imperative we continue to build on our progress rather than turn around and repeal the ACA, which is a giant step backward.

Hillary will also continue her lifelong work of advocating for the health of women, seniors, and veterans. She has been an ardent supporter of women's reproductive health and will continue to ensure that all women and girls are able to make their own health decisions with their doctors. She will protect Medicare and rein in drug companies who are bankrupting our seniors.[9] Hillary has always paid special attention to the health needs of veterans and will continue to demand returning veterans get the care they need, especially those who suffer from mental health issues like PTSD.[10]

The Republicans have made repeal of the ACA their rallying cry in the hopes that denouncing the policy that provided affordable coverage to millions of Americans will be politically advantageous. The Party has tried at least 56 times to repeal Obamacare, even after the US Supreme Court upheld its validity.[11] The GOP has even shut down the government in an attempt to defund the law, and will likely attempt to do so again.[12] Yet Republicans refuse to pursue bipartisan solutions, nor are they able to articulate adequate alternative plans of their own.[13] If the GOP could have its way, millions of Americans would be uninsured and insurance companies would still be allowed to abuse their power and charge premiums that American families simply can't afford.

Starting over means going backward to the days when insurance companies were in charge and millions of Americans could not afford basic health insurance for themselves and their families. Hillary will not let that happen and will work to improve on the ACA and ensure that the right to healthcare is protected and upheld in America.

# 19 ► She Will Pick Fair and Just Supreme Court Nominees

*"In short, in a single term, the Supreme Court could demolish pillars of the progressive movement. And as someone who has worked on every single one of these issues for decades, I see this as a make-or-break moment. If you care about the fairness of elections, the future of unions, racial disparities in universities, the rights of women, or the future of our planet, you should care about who wins the presidency and appoints the next Supreme Court justices."*

—Hillary Clinton[1]

Hillary knows that the very future of the Supreme Court is at stake in this election. The next president of the United States will decide who will sit on the bench, and therefore protect and defend some of the most critical issues of our time—issues surrounding reproductive health, voting rights, healthcare, campaign finance reform, and LGBT rights, to name a few. With the death of Justice Scalia and the fact that by the end of the next president's first term, three other justices will be over the age of 80, the next president of the United States will likely nominate three, or even four justices, dramatically shifting the composition of the Court.[2] Given that Supreme Court justices are appointed for life and are serving longer terms than ever before, the next president's Supreme Court picks will have a profound influence for generations to come. Hillary is committed to ensuring that Supreme Court nominees are fair and just and will protect the constitutional principles of liberty and equality for all.

A majority of Americans do not trust Donald Trump to make nominations to the Supreme Court, and by double digit margins trust Hillary more than Trump with the duty of picking a Supreme Court justice.[3] Given what is at stake, it is no surprise that Americans are worried about who will nominate future Supreme Court justices.

Some of the issues that will likely be decided in coming years include the following:

- Safeguarding legal abortion: Republicans have ramped up their efforts to make it harder for women to access safe and legal abortions and want to overturn *Roe v. Wade*. Hillary will ensure the justices she nominates respect women's reproductive freedom.
- Protecting voting rights: Republicans want to make it harder for people to vote, and have passed multiple laws that impose barriers to participation for people of color, low-income voters, and seniors. Hillary will ensure her Supreme Court picks believe in a democracy where all voters have an equal voice.
- The freedom to marry and LGBT rights: Last year, the Supreme Court ruled in favor of the freedom to marry for gays and lesbians. A Republican president could nominate justices who would reverse that decision, setting back LGBT rights. Hillary will nominate justices who would uphold the law of the land and ensure equality for all.
- Campaign finance reform: The conservative Court ruled in the Citizens United decision that corporations could spend unlimited money to influence elections, greatly exacerbating the money in politics problem. Hillary has pledged to nominate justices who believe in fair campaign finance rules.

The stakes could not be higher, and the impact the next president will have on the Supreme Court could not be greater. President Obama's successor will have the power to pick justices who will either safeguard and advance Americans' fundamental rights and freedoms, or roll them back, restricting liberty and justice for generations to come. Hillary will nominate Supreme Court justices who will uphold the core American values of equality, freedom, fairness, and opportunity. Under Hillary's leadership, the United States Supreme Court will be an agent of progress that will bring our country forward, not backward.

# 20 ▶ She Will Fight for Fair Taxes for American Families

*"Instead of an economy built by every American, for every American, we were told that if we let those at the top pay lower taxes and bend the rules, their success would trickle down to everyone else. What happened? Well, instead of a balanced budget with surpluses that could have eventually paid off our national debt, the Republicans twice cut taxes for the wealthiest, borrowed money from other countries to pay for two wars, and family incomes dropped. You know where we ended up."*

—Hillary Clinton[1]

Hillary knows our tax code is rigged in favor of the wealthiest Americans and corporations. There is something fundamentally wrong when the secretary pays a higher tax rate than the multimillionaire corporate CEO she works for.[2] Hillary also believes that corporations need to pay their fair share of taxes just as working American families do. Reforming our tax code is part of Hillary's overall plan to grow our economy and help American families get ahead and stay ahead.

Hillary has always been a strong supporter of cutting taxes for American families and closing tax loopholes so that the wealthy and big corporations pay their fair share. As senator, she voted against President Bush's tax plans[3] in 2001 and 2003, which shifted the tax burden from the wealthy to middle class and working Americans. Recent analyses point to the Bush tax cuts as drivers of economic inequality.[4] Hillary also fought for the inclusion of an amendment that would have increased tax deductions for college tuition, making education more affordable for millions of Americans.[5]

During her 2008 presidential campaign, Hillary spoke out in favor of closing the "carried interest" loophole that allows hedge fund managers and other Wall Street executives to pay a much lower percentage of money owed in taxes compared to regular Americans earning the same amount.[6] Hillary wants to stop rigging the rules to work for Wall Street "so there can be prosperity on Main Street."[7]

As president, Hillary will implement a tax plan that contains targeted cuts and credits to help middle-class families pay for higher education and allow Americans working paycheck to paycheck to keep more of their money. As part of her New College Compact, she is calling for extending a tax cut of up to $2,500 per student to help deal with college costs.[8] She will also provide tax relief to the engines of America's economy—small businesses—and encourage their growth by cutting red tape, expanding access to capital, and expanding access to new markets.[9]

Hillary will also close the loopholes allowing the super wealthy to pay a lower tax rate than the workers who clean their offices pay. Making the top 1 percent pay their fair share of taxes would generate $157 billion in revenue in the first year alone, which will fund Hillary's education initiatives, including her plans to make college more affordable and provide universal pre-K to children.[10] Her plan promotes long-term investment over short-term profiteering, which will reduce our deficit, expand our economy, and incentivize growth.

Hillary's plan to make the tax code fair and work for all American families is far different from the GOP's strategy to cut taxes for the wealthy and corporations.[11] Hillary's plan will put America on the path towards fiscal responsibility and long-term economic growth. By reducing burdens on American families and making the top earners pay their fair share, we will be able to fund vital programs that will contribute to a stronger economy and stronger families.

# 21 ➤ She Will Create a Criminal Justice System that Works

*"We can heal our wounds. We can restore balance to our justice system and respect in our communities. And we can make sure that we take actions that are going to make a difference in the lives of those who for too long have been marginalized and forgotten."*

—Hillary Clinton[1]

Hillary knows that the criminal justice system in America is broken, and we need common sense solutions to create a system that is efficient, fair, and just. The United States is home to only 5 percent of the world's population, but houses nearly a quarter of the global prison population, the vast majority of whom are nonviolent offenders.[2] Housing the prison population comes at a significant cost to taxpayers—a whopping $63.4 billion a year.[3] In some states, like New York and California, housing just one prisoner can cost up to $60,000 a year, the salary of a teacher or a firefighter.[4]

There are also alarming disparities across the justice system: African American men are far more likely to be stopped and searched by police, charged with crimes, and sentenced to longer prison terms compared to their white counterparts.[5] Our criminal justice system is out of balance, and as a result communities and families across America suffer. Reforming our system is part of Hillary's plan to strengthen communities, move our country forward, and ensure every American has a fair shot at living up to their potential.

Throughout her career, Hillary has recognized the importance of reforming our criminal justice system. In the Senate, Hillary stood up against racial profiling when she was a member of the Senate and was an original co-sponsor of the End Racial Profiling Acts of 2001 and 2004.[6] She has also supported alternatives to mandatory sentencing, like drug treatment programs instead of incarceration, as well as "second chance" programs designed to keep young African Americans out of prison.[7]

As president, Hillary will introduce several reforms aimed at making the criminal justice system more efficient, fair, and just. Her goal is to end the era of mass incarceration by reforming mandatory minimum sentences for nonviolent offenses. Part of her plan enables judges to enact fairer punishments and significantly reduce the percentage of prisoners who are being held for victimless crimes and those who are in prison while awaiting trial because they cannot afford bail. She will also reduce penalties for nonviolent drug offenders and work to focus law enforcement resources on violent crimes rather than drug possession, especially marijuana.[8] As Hillary says of the nonviolent offender population: "Keeping them behind bars does little to reduce crime, but it does a lot to tear apart families and communities."[9]

Hillary will also help prisoners in their transition back to civilian life. She wants to create more opportunities for those who re-enter their communities, and will take executive action to prohibit employers from asking about an applicant's criminal record prior to considering their qualifications.[10] Hillary will also expand treatment for those who suffer from drug addiction to ensure that offenders won't slide back into abuse after they are released. Studies have demonstrated that expanding these initiatives will cut down on recidivism and aid a greater number of former inmates in their efforts to reclaim their lives and rejoin their families and communities.[11]

Hillary will also rebuild trust between police officers and the communities they serve. She wants every police department to require that their officers wear body cameras while on active duty. Hillary favors community-oriented police strategies that are designed to better familiarize police departments with the communities under their jurisdiction and stress cooperation and shared responsibility over punishment and fear.[12]

Finally, Hillary knows that creating economic opportunity is essential to preventing most crime in the first place. Hillary's number one priority is to raise incomes for American families, but she also has specific plans to ensure that people most at risk of falling into the criminal justice system have a fair shot. She has a plan to expand educational opportunities for African Americans by providing assistance to historically black colleges and universities, and incentivize them to fund the education of students from lower income families.[13] Her economic plan also includes a minimum wage increase, and policies that will promote equal pay, paid family leave, and affordable child care—all of which will improve the lives of African American workers.[14]

Fixing the criminal justice system and restoring balance to it will be among Hillary's top priorities. She is not afraid to have the difficult conversation about race and justice in America, and in fact she insists that, as a country, we examine these hard truths and change our policies accordingly so that every American has a fair shot.

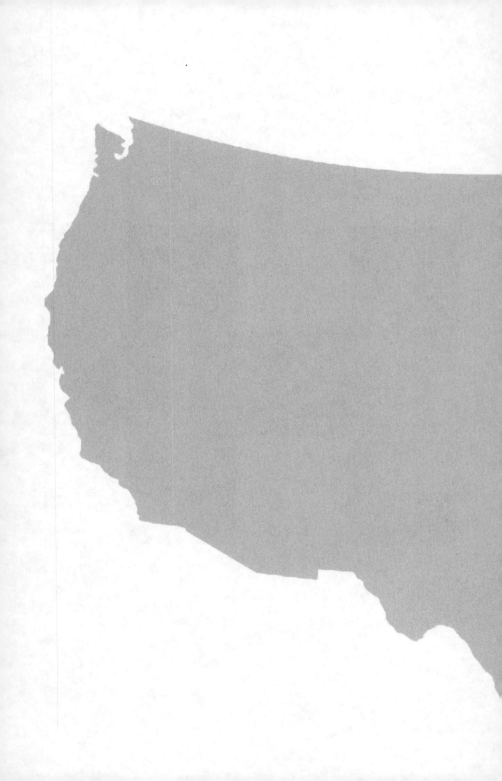

# Human Dignity

# 22 ▶ She Believes in a Roadmap to Citizenship

*"We have to keep families together. We have to treat everyone with dignity and compassion, uphold the rule of law, and respect our heritage as a nation of immigrants striving to build a better life."*
*—Hillary Clinton*[1]

America is a nation of values, founded on an idea that all men and women are created equal, and that all people have rights, no matter what they look like or where they come from. Hillary believes that how we as a country treat new immigrants reflects our commitment to the values that define us as Americans. It's not about what you look like or where you were born that makes you American, it's how you live your life and what you do that defines you here in this country. That's why Hillary believes that all Americans who contribute to this country, our communities, and our economy deserve a common sense immigration process, one that includes a roadmap for people who aspire to be citizens.

Americans of all political persuasions agree that our current immigration process is broken and that we need to create a system that includes a roadmap to citizenship—more than 3 in 5 Americans believe we should allow illegal immigrants to remain in the United States and become US citizens if they meet certain requirements.[2] Hillary has a long history of fighting for legislation and policies that would address our country's broken system and create a common sense immigration process. She co-sponsored the DREAM Act, which would allow immigrants who came to the US as children to become citizens.[3] She has also fought continuously for comprehensive immigration reform, arguing that its passage would ensure families could stay together: "It is time to take all the rhetoric about family values and put it into action and show that we mean what we say when we talk about putting families first."[4]

She has also advocated for policies that would improve the lives of immigrants already in the United States. She introduced and helped pass the Legal Immigrant Children's Health Improvement Act, which ensured access to healthcare for immigrant children and pregnant women. This legislation was widely praised on both sides of the aisle for cutting the number of uninsured children living in poverty in half.[5] She has also advocated for programs for immigrants that would provide job training and English language instruction."[6]

As president, Hillary will ensure that our broken immigration system is fixed once and for all, and that immigrants who contribute to our communities and economy will have a roadmap to citizenship. Her plan rewards hardworking immigrants who uphold American values and would deport violent criminals who harm our country.[7] It is a much more sensible approach than those promoted by conservative Republicans that call for mass deportation of the more than 11 million undocumented immigrants in the United States[8] and the banning of all Muslims.[9] The Republican alternative will cost taxpayers hundreds of billions of dollars and disrupt our economy, which relies on the labor and skills of hardworking immigrants.[10] Even more "moderate" Republican proposals that call for an enforcement-only approach have been discredited as futile—the United States has spent almost $200 billion on enforcement policies since 1986, yet the number of immigrants crossing our borders has tripled.[11] The Republican way is backward, out of touch, and simply not working.

Studies have shown that plans like Hillary's would significantly boost the American economy by generating up to $5 billion in tax revenue from new citizens and raising the earnings of American workers.[12] A common sense immigration process would ensure that employers who exploit illegal immigrant workers would be held accountable so wages for all workers are fair.[13]

The need for immigration reform is clear, and not only will Hillary's common sense immigration process improve the US economy, it will also bring our country closer to the core American values that define us as Americans—opportunity, equality, and respect for the dignity of all human beings.

# 23 ▶ She Will Fight to Eliminate Violence Against Women

*"In whatever form it takes, gender-based violence is an intolerable violation of human dignity."*

—Hillary Clinton[1]

Every day, women in America are beaten, raped, or murdered, often by an intimate partner. One in three women has experienced severe physical violence in her lifetime, one in five women has been raped, and three or more women are murdered everyday by their boyfriend or husband.[2] Worldwide, 35 percent of women have survived physical or sexual violence.[3] Hillary believes that these statistics constitute a gross violation of human rights, and that as a country we can no longer stand by as women and girls are battered, violated, and killed. Violence against women is neither a private problem, nor a family problem. It is a public health problem that necessitates comprehensive policy solutions and action. As president, Hillary will address this crisis head on and fight to ensure that all human beings are able to live their lives with dignity, free from the threat of physical or sexual violence.

Creating a world where women are free from the threat of violence is not only the right thing to do, it's the smart thing to do in order to build healthy, strong communities. When lost work productivity, healthcare and criminal justice costs are taken into account, violence against women costs the United States $8.3 billion per year.[4] Confronting violence and ensuring that women can live up to their full potential will lead to a stronger, more productive country that will benefit all American families.

Hillary has spent her career championing issues facing women and girls, including violence against women around the world. Her well-known and well-received 1995 speech at the UN's Fourth World Conference on Women in Beijing denounced violence against women and declared that women's rights are human rights, a groundbreaking statement at that point in time.[5] That same year, Hillary created the Department of Justice's Office of Violence Against Women.[6] She also fought for the landmark federal legislation, the Violence Against Women Act (VAWA), which gave power to the federal government to punish perpetrators of domestic violence and support survivors and their children.[7]

As senator, Hillary introduced and fought for several pieces of legislation addressing violence against women and girls. She was one of the first legislators to seriously address the problem of violence against women in the military, and introduced a bill that would ensure survivors of rape and sexual assault have access to the healthcare services they need.[8] As secretary of state, Hillary put the spotlight on sexual violence around the world, especially in conflict zones. In conjunction with the Department of Defense and USAID, she coordinated the development of the US National Action Plan on Women, Peace, and Security, which focused on stopping rape and sexual violence in war zones.[9]

Ensuring respect for the dignity of all human beings is one of Hillary's core values, and ending violence against women and girls will be a top priority of her presidency. A key part of Hillary's plan involves tackling rape on college campuses, where as many as one in four women are sexually violated.[10] Hillary's plan will ensure every college campus offers survivors the confidential care and support they need, like counseling and healthcare services. She will also work to increase transparency and fairness throughout campus disciplinary proceedings, to ensure that perpetrators are held accountable. Finally, Hillary will promote rape prevention education on campus as well as in high schools across the country.[11]

As part of her ongoing efforts to end rape and sexual assault in the military, Hillary supports Senator Kirsten Gillibrand's plan to make military sexual assault proceedings more fair and transparent.[12] In a work environment where as many as one in three women experience rape, sexual assault, and sexual harassment, Hillary's attention to military sexual assault is needed to address this crisis and ensure criminal rapists are brought to justice.[13]

Hillary's forty-year record of standing up for women and girls demonstrates her strong commitment to ending violence against women and ensuring the respect and dignity of all human beings. Creating a world where women and girls can live free from the threat of violence will ensure that women can participate fully in society and contribute to their communities and to their country.

# 24 ▶ She Believes That Black Lives Matter

*"Black lives matter. Everyone in this country should stand firmly behind that. We need to acknowledge some hard truths about race and justice in this country, and one of those hard truths is that racial inequality is not merely a symptom of economic inequality. Black people across America still experience racism every day. Since this campaign started, I've been talking about the work we must do to address the systemic inequities that persist in education, in economic opportunity, in our justice system. But we have to do more than talk—we have to take action."*

—Hillary Clinton[1]

Hillary believes that in order for our country to move forward, we must acknowledge some hard truths about race in America. Recent incidents involving the deaths of African Americans at the hands of police have illuminated the most devastating manifestations of racism in America. Young black men are 21 times more likely to be killed by police than their white counterparts,[2] yet are twice as likely as whites to be unarmed.[3] While the lost lives of unarmed black people killed by police represent racism at its worst in our country, systemic injustices penetrate our society—in education, the workplace, and the criminal justice system. Hillary believes that as Americans, we need to do better.

Hillary's record demonstrates her longstanding commitment to eradicating the inequality that infects American institutions. She has spoken out against the alarming disparities across the justice system. African American men are far more likely to be stopped and searched by police, charged with crimes, and sentenced to longer prison terms compared to whites.[4] In the Senate, Hillary stood up against racial profiling and was an original co-sponsor of the End Racial Profiling Acts of 2001 and 2004.[5] She has also supported alternatives to mandatory sentencing, like drug treatment programs instead of incarceration, as well as "second chance" programs designed to keep young African Americans out of the criminal justice system.[6] Hillary also proposed a program to train police officers to work in partnership with communities to prevent violent crimes, thereby improving the relations between African American communities and police officers.[7]

As president, Hillary will go even further to address racism in America and provide equal opportunities for African Americans. She will ensure police departments across the country require their officers to wear body cameras. This policy will not only promote transparency and build trust in communities, but also will deter unnecessarily aggressive policing and potential abuse. She also will end the policies that contribute to mass incarceration of African Americans by reforming mandatory minimum sentences for low-level crimes and promoting drug and mental health treatment over prison for non-violent offenders. These policies will significantly reduce the disproportionate criminalization of blacks in America.

Hillary knows that in order to truly address racism in America, we must address the economic roots of inequality. As she said: "You cannot talk about smart policing and reforming the criminal justice system if you also don't talk about what's needed to provide economic opportunity; better educational chances for young people; more support to families so they can do the best jobs they are capable of doing to help support their own children."[8] She has a plan to expand educational opportunities for African Americans by providing assistance to historically black colleges and universities, incentivizing them to fund the education of students from lower income families.[9] Her economic plan also includes a minimum wage increase, and policies that will promote equal pay, paid family leave, and affordable child care—changes that will improve the lives of African American workers, especially women of color who are much more likely to live in poverty.[10]

Hillary's willingness to take on racism in America and speak truth to what is a disgraceful lingering heritage of our country reflects her strong commitment to ensuring every American can live up to their God-given potential, and that every human being is treated with dignity.

# 25 She Cares About Our Veterans

*"I think it is the highest obligation of the President, who is also our Commander-in-Chief, to take care of those who have served our nation."*

—Hillary Clinton[1]

Hillary believes that as a country, we have a responsibility to ensure the 21.8 million brave men and women veterans[2] who have risked their lives to defend our country and the principles on which it stands get the support and respect they deserve. But we as a country are not doing as good of a job as we can to take care of our vets. On any given night, nearly 50,000 veterans are homeless,[3] more than half a million are unemployed,[4] and 22 vets take their own lives every day.[5] Hillary believes that veterans have served America, and it's time their country serves them. For many service members, the war is not over when they return home, and Hillary is committed to ensuring veterans receive the healthcare, benefits, and support they need to successfully reintegrate into civilian life and contribute to our communities.

Hillary understands the tremendous sacrifice servicemen and women make to America and her history demonstrates her commitment to veterans. The daughter of a World War II vet,[6] Hillary has a long history of introducing, sponsoring, and advocating for legislation intended to help veterans and their families. In 2006, she introduced the Heroes at Home Act, which helped family members care for veterans with traumatic brain injuries or PTSD.[7] She also teamed up with Republican Senator Lindsey Graham (SC) to expand healthcare access to members of the National Guard and Reservists.[8] As a member of the Senate Armed Services Committee, Hillary worked to expand healthcare coverage and assistance to veterans suffering from mental health issues.[9]

One of Hillary's most significant accomplishments was the spearheading of legislation that helped veterans continue their education after service. The 21st Century GI Bill of Rights, signed into law in 2008, provides extensive financial assistance to veterans seeking higher education opportunities after they have completed their service. The law eliminated many of the barriers that precluded veterans returning from active duty in Iraq and Afghanistan from exploring these opportunities, such as the $1,200 program enrollment fee veterans previously had to pay out of pocket.[10] Hillary fought for this legislation in order to ensure veterans have access to educational opportunities that will prepare them for the economy of tomorrow.

In the spirit of continuing her dedication to veterans and their families, Hillary recently announced a plan to close loopholes that enable for-profit colleges to target veterans and exploit them for their own financial gain.[11] She also wants to expand the Military Lending Act, which protects veterans from predatory lenders.[12]

Hillary will also work toward solving some of the most critical issues facing veterans today, including the high rates of suicide. Although the VA has made progress toward addressing this issue, Hillary believes we can do more to help our vets. She will expand access to treatment for substance abuse and mental health issues, particularly post-traumatic stress, traumatic brain injury, and other invisible wounds of war.[13] Ensuring that veterans get the mental health services they need will lead to stronger, healthier communities around the country. And providing educational opportunities to veterans will not only address the problem of unemployment and under-employment among this population, but will empower veterans to use their skills and give back to their communities and country.

The Republicans talk a lot about doing more for our veterans, but their policy proposals include devastating cuts to funding that our veterans rely on.[14] Our economy and our country will be stronger when veterans are healthy and productive, and Hillary will fulfill our country's duty to protect, support, and honor those who have served our nation.

# 26 ▶ She Will Combat Gun Violence

*"It is just beyond my comprehension that we are seeing these mass murders happen again and again and again. And as I have said, we have got to get the political will to do everything we can to keep people safe."*
—Hillary Clinton[1]

Gun violence in America infects communities everywhere and has taken a massive toll on our country. On average, 82 Americans lose their lives at the hands of a gun every day, and 7 of those Americans are children.[2] Shootings in schools, churches, and on street corners have no place in a civilized society, and Hillary will take decisive action to strengthen our gun laws and keep weapons out of the hands of criminals and the mentally ill. While the Republicans are standing up for the NRA and gun lobby, Hillary will stand up for the safety and security of American families and work tirelessly to combat gun violence in our communities.

Hillary has a history of working toward sensible gun control legislation aimed at ensuring guns do not fall into the hands of people that will perpetrate violence. As First Lady, she supported her husband's signing of the Brady Bill, which mandates federal background checks for gun sales.[3] She also supported the passage of the federal assault weapons ban that was in effect for 10 years.[4] Also as First Lady, Hillary convened the White House Summit on School Violence after the Columbine massacre,[5] which brought stakeholders on both sides of the table to come up with solutions to keep kids safe. As senator, she supported a number of bills that would close loopholes in existing regulations, such as preventing unauthorized gun sales via the internet.[6]

Hillary has already released a comprehensive plan to combat gun violence in America once she is president. The core of her plan involves closing loopholes in existing laws and cracking down on gun dealers who aren't following the law.[7] Thirty-eight percent of federally licensed dealers refused to comply with existing gun laws in 2011, but only 71 licenses were revoked by the ATF.[8] Hillary will be aggressive in holding these gun dealers accountable. She will also expand background checks on gun purchases, a policy that many Republicans oppose, yet more than 9 in 10 Americans favor.[9]

Hillary recognizes that addressing our broken mental health system must be part of the solution to reining in gun violence, and her plan incorporates improving mental health facilities and treatment, as well as strengthening regulations that prevent people with certain mental illnesses from purchasing guns.[10]

The horrors of gun violence in America beg for common sense solutions that will keep our communities and children safe. For far too long, political leaders have wavered on this issue, failing to exert strong leadership or prioritize combating gun violence in America. Hillary believes we should do more than just shake our heads; as a country, it is our responsibility to act and stand up for the safety of American families. As she puts it: "This is not just tragic. We don't just need to pray for people. We need to act and we need to build a movement."[11] Hillary is ready and willing to combat gun violence in America and stand up to the National Rifle Association lobbyists and their Republican allies who have rejected even the most benign measures to fight gun violence. She will ensure that our laws and policies put the safety and security of American families first.

**She Will Fight for LGBT Rights in the US and Worldwide**

*"But we know that the struggle for LGBT rights doesn't end with today's triumph. As love and joy flood our streets today, it is hard to imagine how anyone could deny the full protection of our laws to any of our fellow Americans—but there are those who would. So while we celebrate the progress won today, we must stand firm in our conviction to keep moving forward. While we celebrate today, our work won't be finished until every American can not only marry, but live, work, pray, learn and raise a family free from discrimination and prejudice. We cannot settle for anything less."*

> —Hillary Clinton, in a statement on the Supreme Court same-sex marriage decision[1]

Hillary believes that LGBT rights are human rights, and human rights are LGBT rights. That's why she supported the US Supreme Court's decision guaranteeing same sex marriage, remarking of the decision that "equality triumphed, and America triumphed."[2] But LGBT rights are about more than the freedom to marry, and span the gamut of protections that every American—and every human being—should be afforded, including rights and protections in the workplace, in housing, and in schools. Hillary will fight to ensure that all Americans can live, learn, pray, raise a family, and work free from discrimination. Strong families, no matter their sexual orientation, are the bedrock of a strong America.

Hillary has fought for equality for all Americans throughout her career, and has been a vocal advocate for LGBT rights and protections. As senator, she co-sponsored and supported bills designed to prohibit employee discrimination on the basis of sexual orientation.[3] She also co-sponsored the Matthew Shepard Hate Crimes Prevention Act, which allows violence against LGBT individuals to be investigated as hate crimes.[4] She also advocated to end restrictions that blocked LGBT couples from adopting children, because she knows that it is in the best interests of children that all qualified adults who have room in their hearts and homes are permitted to adopt, and are treated fairly in the process.

As secretary of state, Hillary continued her support of LGBT rights, both in America and around the world. She partnered with other nations at the UN to approve the first-ever resolution affirming that LGBT rights are human rights.[5] She also ended State Department rules that denied same-sex couples and their families equal rights.[6] In an effort to ensure transgender individuals are treated with dignity and respect as well, Hillary changed the State Department's policy so that transgender individuals' passports can reflect their true gender.[7]

Moving forward, Hillary has outlined a plan that would ensure LGBT rights and protections are extended across society. In July 2015, she announced her support for the Equality Act of 2015,[8] which expands the 1964 Civil Rights Act to include comprehensive protection from discrimination for LGBT individuals in the areas of credit, education, employment, housing, federal financial assistance, jury service, and public accommodations.[9] Many consider the Equality Act the next big fight for LGBT rights,[10] and Hillary is prepared to take this fight on and win so that all Americans can live their lives free from discrimination.

Hillary also opposes Arkansas and Indiana's Religious Freedom Restoration Acts that allow public businesses to discriminate against LGBT customers, and would oppose similar measures touted by Republicans that would allow LGBT discrimination in other states.[11]

Hillary's plan to move LGBT equality forward in this country and around the world is in stark contrast with the GOP agenda to roll back LGBT rights. Candidates for the Republican nomination oppose what is now the law of the land—the Supreme Court decision guaranteeing marriage equality—and some have even called for legislation that would effectively overturn the decision.[12] The Republican Party is out of touch with the nearly two-thirds of Americans who support the Supreme Court decision[13] and the three in five 2016 voters who say they would be less likely to support a presidential candidate who opposes non-discrimination protections for LGBT people.[14]

In her statement on the Supreme Court decision guaranteeing marriage equality, Hillary said that the decision "represents our country at its best: inclusive, open, and striving towards true equality."[15] Hillary's strong support of marriage equality represents a stark contrast to Republicans like Ted Cruz, who believes individual states should ignore the Supreme Court decision as unconstitutional,[16] and Donald Trump, who said he would appoint justices who would overturn the decision.[17]

Ensuring that all Americans are treated equally and have a fair shot regardless of their sexual orientation is not only the right thing to do, it's the American thing to do. As a country, we are at our strongest when we live up to our ideals of equality and opportunity for all American citizens, and Hillary will make sure that our country—and the world—continues to march forward to the day when all LGBT people can live their lives freely and openly, without the threat of violence or discrimination.

# 28 ▶ She Will Take Care of Our Seniors

*"Our seniors are caught between the soaring costs of care, the desire not to be a burden to their families, and the fear of hurting themselves or others because they are living without the care they need. It's time for a new beginning—and a new approach to helping Americans grow old with dignity. Our seniors deserve our love, our respect, and our care."*
—Hillary Clinton[1]

Hillary believes that supporting American families means taking care of our seniors. The elderly are among the most vulnerable in our country, and we need to make sure we have laws in place that both protect them and ensure they are able to live their lives with dignity. Importantly, we also need to look forward—to the needs of the coming generation—and work to support and provide resources to the family members that care for their older relatives.

Hillary has a strong record of supporting seniors and their families. She has been a staunch defender of Social Security and Medicare throughout her career—as senator, she opposed the Bush administration's plan to privatize Social Security,[2] saying of the policy, "Social Security is one of the greatest inventions in American democracy, and I will do everything possible to protect and defend it."[3] And because she believes seniors are entitled to affordable, accessible healthcare, Hillary voted to override President Bush's veto of Medicare expansion.[4]

Hillary also has a history of standing up to drug companies so that seniors can afford the life-saving prescriptions they need. In the Senate, she voted for a bill that would allow Medicare to negotiate lower prescription drug prices with pharmaceutical companies.[5]

As president, Hillary will stand up to Republicans who want to ravage the Social Security and Medicare benefits seniors have paid into all their lives and were promised.[6] Hillary will also work to support senior women who can suffer financially when their spouses die, as they often face a steep benefit cut. Hillary wants to change the rules to limit how much Social Security benefits are allowed to drop so that the death of a spouse does not mean financial hardship or falling into poverty.[7]

Hillary knows that we need to address the caregiving crisis in our country. Nineteen million seniors need daily care, and that number is expected to double by 2050.[8] But many families cannot afford quality in-home care and need help. Hillary's plan looks toward the future, and addresses the caregiving crisis head-on, to ensure that all American families are supported and can get ahead. She will provide tax relief to those who need it, including a $6,000 tax credit to help families offset the costs of caregiving.[9] She will also fight to ensure American workers have paid family leave, so they can take care of their older relatives without having to worry about losing their jobs or wages.[10]

For Hillary, supporting seniors and their caregivers is an essential component of her plan to strengthen American families everywhere. She will fight to ensure families have the support they need to ensure their elder relatives live their lives with dignity and security.

# 29 ▶ She Will Fix Our Broken Mental Health System

*"Helping more people with an addiction or a mental health problem get help is a family issue."*

—Hillary Clinton[1]

In any given year, 61.5 million, or 1 in 4, Americans experience a mental illness, and 1 in 17 lives with a debilitating disorder like schizophrenia, bipolar disorder, or major depression.[2] The majority of those who suffer from mental health issues never get treated, and the consequences for our country are dire, leading to high rates of homelessness, substance abuse, suicides, and violence. About 60 percent of perpetrators of mass shootings in the United States since 1970 displayed symptoms of a major mental illness.[3] Hillary believes that the broken mental health system in America constitutes a top priority public health problem, one that is harming our communities and literally killing our children. As president, Hillary will address this crisis and make sure that Americans who need help can get it.

Hillary has been committed to addressing mental health issues throughout her career. As senator, she sponsored the Positive Aging Act of 2005, which provided more mental health screenings and treatment services to seniors, who often go undiagnosed and untreated.[4] Hillary also recognized the link between military service and mental health issues, and introduced the Heroes at Home Act of 2006, which provided services for veterans suffering from PTSD and traumatic brain injuries.[5] She also successfully included PTSD family care training programs in the 2007 Defense Budget to make it easier for families of veterans to care for their loved ones.

As president, Hillary will continue her work addressing America's mental health crisis, particularly among veterans, who make up 1 percent of the population but commit 20 percent of suicides.[6] Her proposal to overhaul veterans' healthcare includes substantial funding for mental health treatment services so veterans can heal from the invisible wounds of war. She will also incorporate mental health in her bold plan to combat substance abuse in America. Hillary's proposal includes a $10 billion investment to fight drug and alcohol abuse across the nation, and part of her plan provides increased funding for mental health services, which will help the 9.2 million Americans who have a co-occurring addiction and mental health disorder.[7]

Fixing our broken mental health system is a key component of solving some of the most serious issues in America, including substance abuse, suicide, homelessness, and gun violence. Healthier Americans will lead to stronger families and stronger communities. We need to ensure that every American has access to the care they need, and that mental health is treated for what it is—a public health issue that affects all Americans.

# 30 ▶ She Will Fight for Women Around the World

*"Our mothers and sisters and daughters are on the frontlines of all these battles, but these are not just women's fights. These have to be America's fights and the world's fights. We have to take them on, we have to win them together, and we have to have leaders who recognize that the time has come."*

—Hillary Clinton[1]

In 1995, Hillary declared in her famous speech to the UN Conference in Beijing that "human rights are women's rights, and women's rights are human rights."[2] Her speech galvanized women and human rights activists everywhere and brought much-needed attention to the plight of women and girls around the world. Hillary's speech is symbolic of her unwavering commitment to improving the lives of women in America and around the world. She believes that what is good for women and their families is good for countries, and that promoting women's rights is not only the right thing to do in the name of equality, it's the smart thing to do economically, because it helps economies grow and countries advance.

For forty years, Hillary has worked to end the beating, rape, and harassment of women. She's fought for women's health, including reproductive rights and choice, and she has advocated for smart policies such as equal pay, paid family leave, and affordable child care—policies that not only help women and families get ahead, but also benefit economies. And she has pushed to provide educational opportunities for women and girls both in America and around the world.

As secretary of state, Hillary made women's rights a cornerstone of American foreign policy. She created the position of Ambassador-at-Large for global women's issues[3] and launched the first-ever US strategy on women, peace, and security.[4] She introduced a global health initiative that invested $63 billion to provide maternal and infant health services in partner countries around the world.[5] Hillary also championed programs and facilitated public-private partnerships dedicated to ending gender-based violence and advancing women's economic status.[6] Her initiatives have already reaped results all over the world, like in Tunisia, where women worked together to end violence and create a more inclusive political system;[7] in Saudi Arabia, where women are now allowed to vote and hold political office;[8] and in South Asia, where women are going to school and staying in school.[9] As Hillary explains the utility of focusing foreign policy on women's advancement: "We have really worked to integrate gender issues across the board. Not just stuck over in a corner, but to be considered. We're trying to target a lot of our aid to women because what we have found over many years is that if you help a woman, she helps her family. And then the family and the children are better off."[10]

Despite Hillary's forty-year history of fighting for women and girls, she's just getting started. While the world has witnessed incredible advancement of women's rights everywhere, Hillary considers women's rights "the unfinished business of the 21st century"[11] and will make the empowerment of women and girls a priority as president of the United States. Here at home, she has talked extensively about her plans to ensure equal pay for women, make college debt-free, raise the minimum wage, and expand paid family leave—policies that will help women and their families get ahead and stay ahead. She is also committed to ending violence against women, including on college campuses. Her proposal would provide more health and counseling services to survivors of sexual assault as well as make disciplinary proceedings more fair, so that perpetrators of violence are held accountable for their crimes.[12]

But Hillary will look out toward the world as well, since the status of women worldwide has an impact that reaches beyond countries' individual borders, including to the global economy. She knows that in far too many parts of the world, social, economic, and legal barriers continue to preclude women from reaching their full potential. Hillary wants to address the staggering statistics, such as the fact that one in every three girls in developing countries is married before the age of 18, and laws in 79 countries that still restrict the type of work women can do. Hillary will continue to promote gender equality globally and ensure that women and girls have equal access to education, women are safe from sexual violence, and women have equal economic opportunity. Hillary's approach will promote a more just, secure, and prosperous global community that will benefit us all.

# 31 ▶ She Will Tackle Substance Abuse

*"There are 23 million Americans suffering from addiction. But no one is untouched. We all have family and friends who are affected. We can't afford to stay on the sidelines any longer—because when families are strong, America is strong. Through improved treatment, prevention, and training, we can end this quiet epidemic once and for all."*
—Hillary Clinton[1]

Hillary knows how important addressing the drug addiction crisis is to building strong families and communities. The crisis has remained a quiet epidemic for far too long, plaguing communities around the country. Twenty-three million Americans suffer from addiction, but only 1 person in 10 gets the treatment they need.[2] Substance abuse infects communities, destroys families, and places a serious financial burden on our healthcare and criminal justice systems that taxpayers have to shoulder. Hillary will provide strong leadership on these issues and will take an approach that prioritizes treatment over incarceration for low-level, nonviolent drug abusers. She will address the roots of substance abuse and focus on prevention efforts targeted at children and teens. Hillary's plan will tackle the substance abuse issue head on, strengthening families and communities around the country.

Hillary has a history of addressing substance abuse in communities as part of her criminal justice system reform efforts, as well as in her work on healthcare. As senator, Hillary supported numerous initiatives aimed at providing more treatment options for drug users, instead of incarceration. She co-sponsored the Drug Sentencing Reform and Cocaine Kingpin Trafficking Act of 2007, which eliminated mandatory minimum sentencing for first-time crack cocaine possession. She has also fought for increased funding for mental health services, including for populations at risk of drug addiction, such as returning combat veterans.[3]

Hillary has already proposed several bold initiatives to combat substance abuse in communities around the country, and she will prioritize the advancement of these proposals as president. Her proposal includes a $10 billion investment to fight drug and alcohol abuse across the nation, an unparalleled investment level that is necessary in order to effectively deal with a problem of this magnitude. Her initiative is centered around five goals: 1. empower communities to prevent drug use among teenagers; 2. ensure every person suffering from addiction can obtain comprehensive treatment; 3. ensure that all first responders carry naloxone, which can stop opioid overdoses from becoming fatal; 4. require healthcare providers to receive training in recognizing substance use disorders and to consult a prescription drug monitoring program before prescribing controlled substances; and 5. prioritize treatment over prison for low-level and nonviolent drug offenders, so we can end the era of mass incarceration.[4]

While Hillary believes we must treat drug addiction as a disease and a public health problem, Republicans want to continue to advocate for punitive measures that have proved ineffective. They refuse to shift from their retributive mentality, and have pushed for austere budget cuts to substance abuse treatment and prevention programs.[5] Hillary, on the other hand, wants to provide substance abusers with the resources to heal themselves and become productive members of society. She offers a hand up, while Republicans stick their heads in the sand.

Hillary's plan represents a dramatic shift in the way our country tackles drug addiction. She recognizes that a sizeable investment is necessary in order to provide adequate care for millions of Americans who struggle with addiction, and reduce deaths from overdose. Her plan will help strengthen families and communities and lead to a stronger, more productive country that will benefit all Americans.

# 32 She Will Protect the Rights of Americans with Disabilities

*"So there's a lot of unfinished business—both at home, and around the world. But I personally believe that the progress and the landmark legislation—first on education then broadly opening up transportation and buildings and employment, everything that people should be able to pursue—that that legislation was one of the real highlights of the civil rights and human rights movements in America."*

—Hillary Clinton, on the Americans with Disabilities Act (ADA)[1]

Hillary wants to build a country where no American is left out, and every citizen has an equal opportunity to live up to their potential. That's why protecting and advancing the rights of Americans with disabilities are priorities for Hillary—her America will be one where no one is left behind, including the nearly 57 million—or 1 in 5—Americans who live with a physical or mental disability. Additionally, Hillary will provide support to family members of disabled Americans and empower communities to help advance the rights and opportunities of all Americans regardless of disability status.

Hillary's commitment to human rights began decades ago, and throughout her career she has fought to ensure all Americans can enjoy the full measure of liberty, the full experience of dignity, and the full benefits of humanity. After law school, while most of her colleagues went off to work at big law firms, Hillary joined the Children's Defense Fund, a nonprofit legal advocacy organization. One of her first assignments involved going door-to-door to understand why so many children did not go to school. Hillary and her colleagues found that many schools did not accommodate the needs of disabled children. Her work culminated in the passage of the Individuals with Disabilities Education Act, which guarantees that schoolchildren with disabilities have the right to attend school.[2]

Hillary continued her activism on behalf of disabled Americans in the US Senate where she co-sponsored amendments to the Americans with Disabilities Act (ADA) that provided robust anti-discrimination protections.[3] She also repeatedly introduced legislation that made it easier for veterans returning with psychological disorders such as PTSD to be cared for by their families. Hillary also secured funding for community-based rehabilitation and reintegration programs, so that veterans with disabilities are able to access resources and support in their own communities.[4]

As president, Hillary will continue her dedication to securing human rights for all, including disabled Americans. She will advocate for US ratification of the UN Convention on the Rights of Persons with Disabilities, which codifies that persons with disabilities are no longer simply objects of charity or social protection, but are people with full human rights and the same freedoms as those living without disabilities. She will also improve access to meaningful and gainful employment for people with disabilities. Too many Americans with disabilities continue to be left out of the workforce, or are under-employed in jobs that do not fully allow them to use their talents.

Advancing the rights of disabled Americans will honor our country's commitment to ensuring every American citizen has equal opportunity. America benefits when all Americans can use their talents and contribute to our country. Hillary will ensure that no American is left behind, and that the country we build together respects the dignity of all human beings, including the disabled.

# 33 ▶ She Will Fight for Human Rights Around the World

*"For our democracies to meet the tests ahead, all of our people, not just those of us here, but all of our people, have to believe they too have a stake in our prosperity and our future, no matter where they are from, what they look like, who they worship or who they love."*

—Hillary Clinton[1]

Hillary has spent her entire career fighting for the rights of the most vulnerable groups in society, including women, girls, and children. Her unwavering belief in the dignity of all human beings has inspired her forty-year history of standing up for human rights around the world. While many politicians have given lip service to the promotion of human rights, the difference with Hillary is that she actually has a strong record of taking action and getting things done on these issues.

As First Lady, Hillary demonstrated her commitment to attacking human rights violations across the globe. She was instrumental in pushing her husband to intervene in the war in Bosnia, where tens of thousands of innocent civilians were being massacred.[2,3] She also advocated for humanitarian intervention to stop atrocities—including the rape of children as a war tactic[4]—in places such as Sudan, Libya, and Iraq. And although Hillary has often been described as "hawkish" for her willingness to exert force abroad, she has shown a strong commitment to diplomacy and relationship building, especially in her tenure as secretary of state.

As senator, Hillary pushed for human rights to be a central tenet of American foreign policy. She co-sponsored several Armenian Genocide Resolutions, and repeatedly called on President Bush to recognize the systematic murder of approximately one million people as genocide.[5] She also opposed the Bush Administration's policy of torturing suspected terrorists and declared that torture, "As a matter of policy, cannot be American policy, period."[6]

From the onset of her tenure as secretary of state, Hillary Clinton declared that human rights would be an integral part of American foreign policy.[7] Shortly after taking office, she brought the United States into the UN Human Rights Council, reversing Bush-era policy that rejected American membership. Hillary believes America should take the lead in promoting a global standard of human rights and encouraging nations to abide by these standards. Through this organization and other multilateral institutions, Hillary put teeth into investigating and resolving issues, putting the spotlight on UN member states with deplorable human rights records.[8] She repeatedly castigated China for its suppression of dissidents and intellectuals and its censorship of the internet. She also created a fund for NGOs that provide legal representation and other forms of assistance to vulnerable communities.[9]

Hillary has used her positions as First Lady, senator, and secretary of state to go to bat for those suffering under repression, because she believes that every human being deserves to live a life of dignity. In 2013, she was awarded the Liberty Medal by the National Constitution Center in recognition of her advocacy for human rights over the course of her career in public service. NCC chairman and former Florida Governor Jeb Bush presented Hillary with the award, praising her as having "dedicated her life to serving and engaging people across the world in democracy."[10]

The GOP candidates' stances on human rights are downright frightening. Donald Trump has encouraged the murder of civilian families of terror suspects,[11] while Ted Cruz does not believe waterboarding is torture.[12] As much as Republicans talk about respecting life, their positions on human rights say otherwise. As president, Hillary will respect the dignity of every human being, and will continue to speak out against regimes that deny basic rights and freedoms to their people, and ensure that the United States will stand with the greater international community on promoting universal human rights.

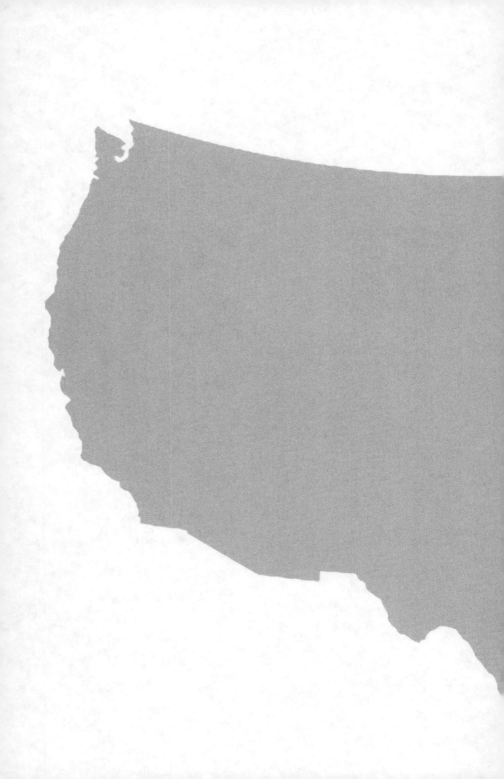

# IV

## Freedom

# 34 ▶ She Will Break ISIS

*"Now, we should have no illusions about how difficult the mission before us really is. We have to fit a lot of pieces together, bring along a lot of partners, move on multiple fronts at once. But if we press forward on both sides of the border, in the air and on the ground, as well as diplomatically, I do believe we can crush ISIS's enclave of terror."*
—Hillary Clinton[1]

No other 2016 presidential candidate is as qualified and prepared as Hillary Clinton is to stop ISIS's reign of terror. She knows that America needs to lead the way to crush the group of radical jihadists who persecute religious and ethnic minorities, behead civilians, murder children, and systematically rape women and girls.[2] The San Bernardino, California attacks that left fourteen people dead were perpetrated by ISIS sympathizers and show the extent to which radicalization has endangered people on our own soil.[3] Under Hillary's leadership, the United States will take decisive steps to destroy the ISIS organization and its ideology of hate and violence.

Hillary has a strong record of taking on terrorism and is not afraid to use American power to defeat terrorists. As secretary of state, she had tremendous influence over President Obama's use of military force, including his decision to carry out the successful raid on Osama bin Laden's compound in Pakistan that resulted in bin Laden's death.[4] Hillary is also credited with convincing Obama to arm moderate Syrian rebels to establish a "credible" opposition that could stand up to Bashar al-Assad, the leader of Syria, as well as ISIS.[5]

Hillary also worked hard to build relationships with other countries to secure a united front against ISIS. She established a global counterterrorism forum of almost 30 nations including China, Russia, India, the EU, and 11 Muslim-majority nations[6] in order to share expertise and mobilize resources against terrorist organizations like ISIS.[7]

As president, Hillary will continue her record of decisively going after terrorists and keeping America safe and secure. Her multilateral, three-pronged approach to crushing ISIS includes the following elements:

1. Defeat ISIS on their home turf in Syria and Iraq: Working with allies in Middle East regions including Egypt, Turkey, and Jordan, Hillary will ramp up airstrikes and put pressure on Baghdad to arm local and regional troops to give them a chance to fight ISIS on the ground.[8]

2. Break up the flow of money and resources ISIS relies on: Hillary has a plan to help opposition forces cut off ISIS's supply lines and put greater pressure on states like Qatar and Saudi Arabia to crack down on organizations and individuals funneling money to these jihadist groups.[9] She also knows how critical it is to fight ISIS's online presence, where many terrorists are spawned. As Hillary has said, "we must deny them virtual territory just as we deny them actual territory."[10]

3. Defend the United States and allies against security threats: Hillary knows that intelligence is among our best defenses against terrorist organizations. She will work to dramatically improve intelligence sharing on terror threats between US and European nations, and encourage European nations to share information with each other.[11] She will also ensure law enforcement have the support and resources they need to pursue credible terrorist threats. Finally, Hillary will establish better and stricter screening of Syrian refugees to ensure no terrorists slip through the cracks and enter our country.[12]

Hillary's approach to defeating ISIS and other terrorist threats is grounded in her experience and knowledge of the world, both of which swamp her opponents. Republicans like Donald Trump want to fight hate with hate and have proposed unworkable, dangerous policies that threaten the security of the American people. As Hillary puts it: "Shallow slogans don't add up to a strategy. Promising to carpet bomb until the desert glows doesn't make you sound strong —it makes you sound like you're in over your head. Bluster and bigotry are not credentials for becoming commander-in-chief."[13]

Breaking ISIS is among the most important reasons to elect Hillary Clinton President of the United States. Her opponents are downright dangerous in their inexperience and misguided policy proposals, and the election of anyone else in 2016 but Hillary Clinton will threaten the security of our country. Under Hillary's leadership, America will be able to lead the way in the fight against terrorist organizations, and will succeed in breaking ISIS once and for all, so that American families can stay safe and secure.

# 35 ➤ She Believes in Using Smart Power Abroad

*"This is what we call smart power—using every possible tool and partner to advance peace and security, leaving no one on the sidelines, showing respect, even for one's enemies, trying to understand and insofar as psychologically possible, empathize with their perspective and point of view, helping to define the problems, determine the solutions. That is what we believe in the 21st century will change—change the prospects for peace."*

—Hillary Clinton[1]

Among Hillary's greatest accomplishments during her tenure as secretary of state is her successful use of smart power—the skillful combination of hard (military) and soft (diplomacy) power. As the Center for Strategic and International Studies defines it: "It is an approach that underscores the necessity of a strong military, but also invests heavily in alliances, partnerships, and institutions at all levels to expand American influence and establish the legitimacy of American action."[2] Hillary is both a hawk and a dove, and her smart, pragmatic approach to foreign policy will make America a safer, stronger, and more prosperous nation.

During Hillary's confirmation hearing, she promoted a strategy of smart power as the "vanguard of foreign policy," and her record shows how successful this strategy was for America. [3] She engaged in back-channel diplomacy with Iran while at the same time successfully leading international negotiations to isolate them. With the understanding that unilateral sanctions were not enough, she created an international coalition that included China and Russia to place crippling sanctions on Iran that eventually brought them to the negotiating table. Without Hillary, the historic deal that blocked Iran's pathway to a nuclear weapon would likely have never happened.[4]

Hillary's successful use of smart power helped repair America's reputation and improve our standing in the world. Research shows that 82 percent of world countries had a more positive view of US influence by the end of Hillary's tenure compared to the beginning.[5] Hillary has the respect of world leaders everywhere, and the relationships she has forged will help America immensely in the foreign policy realm in years to come.

As president, Hillary will continue to use smart power and will work with other countries on major issues facing our country today, including counterterrorism, human rights, and conflict resolution. She will partner with emerging allies who have enormous economic, geopolitical, and social leverage over some of America's greatest rivals. For example, Hillary will reach out to countries like Indonesia, whose strategic location linking the Indian Ocean with the Pacific allows the United States to expand its presence in the region and stave off Chinese expansion.[6]

Hillary will also emphasize the importance of incorporating women of foreign nations in peacekeeping strategies. As she has said, "It's important to underscore this overriding fact: women are not just victims of conflict—they are agents of peace and agents of change."[7] Hillary made numerous efforts as secretary of state to include women as part of security and peacemaking strategies, and will build on this important work in the future.[8]

As president, Hillary will build on her vast foreign policy experience and use smart power to elevate America's position in the world and keep American families safe and secure. Her pragmatic foreign policy vision will take America forward and restore our global leadership.

# 36 ▶ She Will Balance Security and Privacy

*"The balance between the urgent goal of combating terrorism and the safeguarding of our most fundamental constitutional freedoms is not always an easy one to draw. However, they are not incompatible, and unbridled and unchecked executive power is not the answer."*
—Hillary Clinton[1]

Balancing security and privacy is not an easy task, but one Hillary will be committed to as president. Keeping America safe and secure will be one of her top priorities, but doing so cannot come at the cost of sacrificing the fundamental right to personal privacy. The tech community has confidence in Hillary's ability to balance security and privacy,[2] while they have lambasted Republicans like Donald Trump for his blatant disregard of these concerns.[3] Under Hillary's leadership, the American people will stay safe while also enjoying the civil liberties that set America apart.

Hillary has a history of balancing these two fundamental rights throughout her career. In the Senate, she voted for the Patriot Act in 2001[4] as well as its re-authorization in 2006,[5] citing the need to empower law enforcement with the tools they need to go after terrorists. However, she expressed strong reservations about certain provisions in the Act, and introduced an amendment to safeguard civil liberties. As Hillary stated on the Senate floor: "Innocent Americans should not be subjected to these possible intrusions when adequate safeguards can be written into the law, ones that would not sacrifice the utility of these orders as a law enforcement tool. Americans should not have to hope that the government will demonstrate self-restraint in its exercise of this power, nor should they fear that their personal records will be part of a government fishing expedition."[6]

As secretary of state, Hillary promoted a free and open internet. She spoke against other countries who routinely violated their citizens' privacy, saying that the challenges governments face in using intelligence to identify terrorist threats "must not become an excuse for governments to systematically violate the rights and privacy of those who use the internet for peaceful political purposes."[7]

Hillary has often spoken about how she would reform surveillance laws. She supports the USA Freedom Act, which reauthorizes certain Patriot Act provisions that help monitor potential terrorist threats,[8] but also places restrictions on the bulk collection of data from American citizens.[9]

To Hillary, maintaining a free and open internet around the world is a core value,[10] but equally important is blocking ISIS and other terrorist groups from using social media to spread their propaganda and recruit new followers.[11] She has proposed working with Silicon Valley and other large private sector firms to identify and disrupt information networks that foster recruitment or incite violence.[12]

Hillary is up to the tough task of ensuring our laws are balanced to keep America safe while also guarding citizens' liberty and privacy. Our country needs an open and transparent conversation that weighs the importance of privacy with the realities of keeping America safe, and Hillary has proven she is the person to lead that discussion and make the changes we need. Her record shows her ability to strike this delicate balance, and our country and our world will be both safer and freer under Hillary's leadership.

# 37 ▶ She Stands With Israel

*"When it comes to a region full of uncertainty, upheaval, revolution, this much is constant and clear: America and Israel are in it together. This is a friendship that comes naturally to us. Americans honor Israel as a homeland dreamed of for generations and finally achieved by pioneering men and women in my lifetime. We share bedrock beliefs in freedom, equality, democracy, and the right to live without fear. What threatens Israel threatens America, and what strengthens Israel strengthens us."*

— Hillary Clinton[1]

Hillary has shown an unwavering commitment to Israel's security and the importance of maintaining America's strong bond with Israel, our closest friend and our strongest ally in the Middle East. At a time when Israel's enemies are bolder than ever before, it is imperative that the next leader of the United States upholds our dedication to the survival of the Jewish state, the one shining example of democracy in the region, and that's exactly what Hillary will do.

Throughout her career, Hillary has made great efforts to keep Israel safe. As senator, Hillary supported the Israeli government's efforts to prevent terror attacks and promote peace. She was an early supporter of the security fence between Israel and the West Bank that has reduced suicide attacks in Israel significantly in the past decade.[2] In 2006, Hillary co-sponsored the Palestinian Anti-Terrorism Act, a bipartisan law prohibiting foreign assistance to Hamas and affiliated terrorist organizations.[3] Her efforts to weaken and isolate terrorist groups have made both Israel and the United States safer.

As secretary of state, Hillary took a firm stance against Iran, whose leaders routinely call for the destruction of Israel. She formed an international coalition that placed the toughest sanctions on Iran to date.[4] These sanctions proved effective in crippling Iran's economy, and brought them to the negotiating table. Hillary was adamant about protecting Israel from Iranian aggression, warning our enemies that "an attack on Israel would incur massive retaliation from the United States."[5] As president, Hillary will execute the strong, smart leadership our country needs to successfully defend our most valuable ally in the region, thereby keeping the United States safe and secure.

Hillary has promised to deepen our unshakable commitment to Israel's security. As America's next leader, she will renew the US–Israel Memorandum of Understanding, which provides a ten-year commitment from America to provide Israel with the security assistance it needs to maintain the most capable and strongest military in the Middle East.[6] Specifically, she will increase support for rocket and missile defense and push for better technology that will help protect Israel from infiltration by terrorists.[7]

Hillary will also vigorously enforce the nuclear agreement with Iran and will not hesitate to take military action should Iran attempt to obtain a weapon.[8] Hillary is fearless when it comes to protecting our nation and our allies. She will also work with other international allies to put pressure on Iran to withdraw their support for terrorists that threaten Israel and destabilize the region.

Our country needs a leader who will defend and protect our greatest ally in the Middle East, thereby protecting American families at home. Time and time again, Hillary has demonstrated her commitment to keeping Israel secure, and she has the experience, strength, and skills to ensure that Israel and America maintain their partnership.

# 38 ▶ She Will Restore American Leadership in Asia

*"China represents one of the most challenging and consequential bilateral relationships the United States has ever had to manage. This calls for careful, steady, dynamic stewardship, an approach to China on our part that is grounded in reality, focused on results, and true to our principles and interests."*

—Hillary Clinton[1]

Hillary has always been fearless when it comes to standing up to China. One of her most iconic moments was during her 1995 speech in Beijing when she denounced governments that show disrespect for the rights of women, famously declaring that "human rights are women's rights and women's rights are human rights."[2] As president, Hillary Clinton will provide leadership in East Asia at a time when a strong American presence is needed. China continues to bully its neighbors, oppress its own people, and stonewall attempts at mitigating climate change. But Hillary knows that China is also a critical partner to America in areas such as counter-terrorism, nuclear non-proliferation, and trade. As president, Hillary will support our allies in Asia in standing up to China's violations of international law and engage with China to work with America on critical issues facing our world today.

Hillary has called out China for its disrespect of human rights and dignity throughout her career. Her speech in Beijing was inspired by China's policies of forced abortion and sterilization, as well as the widespread practice of female infanticide.[3] As secretary of state, she blasted China for its suppression of religious minorities and its overall hostility toward religious freedom,[4] and continues to criticize China for imprisoning feminist human rights activists.[5] Hillary stands up for human rights around the world, and won't turn a blind eye to China's disregard for them.

Beyond her words, Hillary's actions also demonstrate her tough stance against China as well as her solid commitment to America's Asian allies. As secretary of state, Hillary stood up to China's bullying of their Japanese and Korean neighbors in territory disputes.[6] Seeing that the United States would not back down, eleven other Asian nations came out in support of Hillary's proposal. As Forbes columnist Gordon Chang wrote, "Clinton, in her finest hour as Secretary of State, supplied leadership in Southeast Asia."[7] Her efforts to unite the countries of East Asia paid off, as China backed down from its hawkish stance.

As president, Hillary will engage China constructively. She will ensure that our trade relationship with them is fair and beneficial to America, and will not allow them to flood our markets with cheap goods, and utilize inhumane labor practices to outcompete American businesses.[8] Hillary is also committed to stopping climate change, and will work with China on mutual reduction of greenhouse gas emissions. Finally, Hillary will work with China on mitigating North Korea and working towards a nuclear-free Korean Peninsula.[9] As the only supporter of Kim Jong Un's despotic regime, China can exact a great deal of leverage on them to relinquish their nuclear weapons program. A nuclear-free Korea will de-escalate tensions and deter the proliferation of nuclear weapons in northeast Asia.[10] By simultaneously working with China while also holding them accountable, Hillary will restore American leadership in Asia.

# 39 ▶ She Will Protect Women's Reproductive Health

*"This really isn't complicated. When you attack women's health, you attack America's health."*

—Hillary Clinton[1]

Hillary believes that every woman should have the freedom to make her own healthcare decisions with her family, her faith, and the counsel of her doctor. Freedom means access, and Hillary believes that reproductive health services need to be available to all women everywhere. In order for women to live up to their potential, they need to have the resources to take adequate care of their reproductive health and make the right decisions for themselves and their families. That's why Hillary is a strong defender of Planned Parenthood and will stand up to attacks on women's hard-won rights to make their own healthcare choices.

Hillary has been an ardent supporter of women's reproductive rights throughout her career. As First Lady of Arkansas, Hillary chaired the Rural Health Advisory committee, which expanded reproductive healthcare access to thousands of women in isolated rural communities throughout the state.[2] In the White House, Hillary successfully persuaded her husband to reverse the austere Reagan-era policies toward women's reproductive healthcare, even at the objection of Bill's top advisors.[3]

In the Senate, Hillary fought for years to get emergency contraception approved, on the market, and available to women over the counter.[4] She also teamed up with Harry Reid (D–NV) to introduce the Prevention First Act in 2005, which encouraged comprehensive sexual education and use of contraceptives in an effort to decrease the number of abortions performed.[5] Hillary's relentless work on behalf of women and families in America earned her a 100 percent rating from NARAL during her Senate career.[6]

In the wake of the recent accusations against Planned Parenthood regarding the sale of fetal tissue, Hillary has made it clear that she stands with Planned Parenthood, and will defend the organization and the millions of women and girls who rely on Planned Parenthood's health services for life-saving preventive care, like cancer screenings. Hillary will stand up to Republican attacks, including their efforts to defund the organization. As she said recently: "If this feels like a full-on assault on women's health, that's because it is. When politicians talk about defunding Planned Parenthood, they're talking about blocking millions of women, men and young people from live-saving preventive care."[7]

As president, Hillary will also defend the Affordable Care Act's provision that prevents insurance companies from discriminating against covering women because of their reproductive healthcare needs.[8] She will also nominate Supreme Court justices who will uphold *Roe v. Wade* and protect women's access to reproductive healthcare.[9]

The Republican Party wants to turn back the clock on the rights of women, and bring our country backward, to a time when women's healthcare choices were limited. Republicans like Donald Trump and Ted Cruz would defund Planned Parenthood, and Cruz wants to go as far as prosecuting the organization.[10] In their never-ending War on Women, Republicans in several states have tried to pass restrictive laws that interfere with the relationship between a woman and her doctor by forcing health professionals to provide inaccurate and deceptive information about abortion. Texas has required women seeking abortions to undergo a medically unnecessary ultrasound, and several other states have introduced similar legislation.[11] The Republican Party is not only extreme in their positions on reproductive rights, but they are dogmatic to the point where their actions defy common sense.

In contrast, Hillary wants to provide women and their families with choices and ensure that women and girls all over the country have access to the reproductive health services they need. To Hillary, when women are healthy, America will be healthy, and it is critical to ensure women have the opportunities and access they need to build healthy and productive futures for themselves and their families.

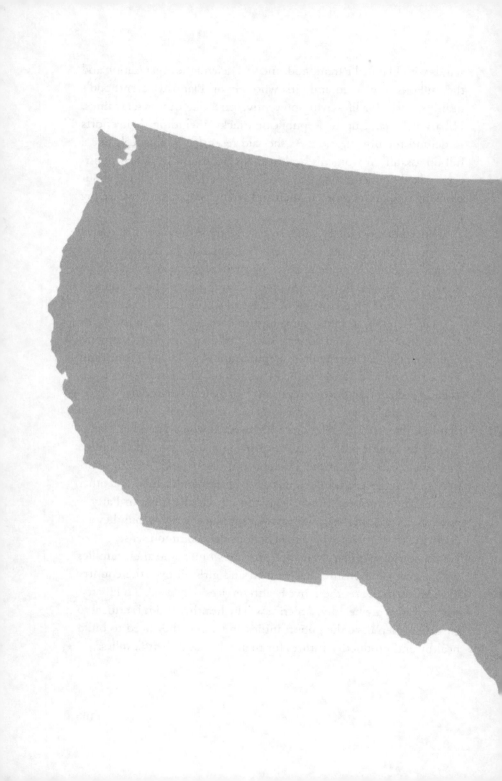

# V

# Perseverance

# 40 ▶ She Is the Most Experienced

*"She's the best change-maker I've ever known."*
—Bill Clinton, on Hillary Clinton[1]

Hillary is by far the most qualified and experienced candidate in the 2016 presidential race, and perhaps even in modern history.[2] Even Republican Senator Marco Rubio admitted that Hillary is undeniably qualified: "If this election is going to be a resume competition, then Hillary Clinton's going to be the next president, because she's been in office and in government longer than anybody else running here tonight."[3] In Clinton's forty years of experience, she has gained the skills and built the relationships necessary to be able to get things done for American families.

Hillary's long history of public service began after she graduated from Yale Law School, when she went to work for the Children's Defense Fund and advocated for the rights of children with disabilities. As First Lady, Hillary fought for and led several key policy initiatives, most famously the healthcare reform legislation. She also worked with Democrats and Republicans to create the Children's Health Insurance Program, which provided healthcare coverage to millions of children in America.[4] In 2000, Hillary began her own political career and became the first woman senator from the state of New York. Among her many accomplishments in the Senate are securing healthcare for 9/11 first responders as well as military members and their families, and helping small businesses use technology to grow.[5]

After running for president in 2008, President Obama asked Hillary to join his cabinet as secretary of state, where she amassed the most foreign policy experience of any candidate in the 2016 race. She was a forceful champion for human rights, internet freedom, and rights and opportunities for women and girls, LGBT people, and young people all around the globe, and has been praised widely for her effectiveness in restoring America's leadership in the world. Even former Republican Secretary of State Henry Kissinger said she "ran the State Department in the most effective way that I've ever seen."[6] Hillary knows the world—she's traveled to 112 countries—and has built strong relationships with leaders around the globe, which has improved America's standing globally.[7]

Some commentators believe Hillary's experience is a liability in an electoral environment that seems to favor outsider candidates, but Hillary's experience—and therefore ability to get things done— is about as outsider as you can get in a political system paralyzed by gridlock and polarization. Our country needs leadership from someone who will prioritize the needs of American families—better jobs and wages, affordable education, equal pay, paid sick and family leave, and an economy that works for the middle class, not just the wealthy and corporations.

Hillary's experience will allow her to lead our country with a steady hand—she knows what she's doing, and will not have to rely on belligerence or bullying to get things done. Using her decades of experience, Hillary will be able to accomplish her goal of ensuring American families get ahead and stay ahead, and that every American has the opportunity to thrive.

**41** **She Can Win**

*"I'm not running to be a President only for those Americans who
already agree with me. I want to be a President for all Americans."*
—Hillary Clinton[1]

Hillary can win the presidency because her vision speaks to the needs
and concerns of American families throughout the country. Her vast
experience in public service and her skills as a leader will aid her in
advancing comprehensive policy solutions to some of our country's
most pressing problems. She will win support from voters all over
the country—including independent and swing voters—and across
demographics, because she is the leader of tomorrow, not yesterday.
She will bring our country forward, not backwards, and ensure all
Americans will realize their potential.

Hillary is a pragmatic progressive who has learned how to get
things done in government, and her decades of experience building
relationships on both sides of the aisle will help her do just that. It
should come as no surprise, then, that poll after poll show American
voters believe Hillary is the most qualified, experienced, and strongest leader in the race.[2] With Republicans in charge, the gridlock that
paralyzes Washington will only get worse, with leaders who want to
divide, not unite, America.

The demographics of the American electorate increasingly favor
Democratic candidates, especially in presidential elections when
core elements of the Democratic coalition—millennials, unmar-
ried women, and people of color—are more likely to turn out.[3]
Presidential candidates must appeal to this emerging electorate of
voters, who will make up the majority of voters for the first time in
2016.[4] Early polls indicate that Hillary already wins the emerging
electorate against Republican contenders, and by wide margins—for
example, in a hypothetical match-up against Trump, voters under

35 would choose Clinton by a crushing 52 to 19 percent, a preference that holds across demographic lines.[5] The emerging electorate supports Hillary and the Democratic Party because they know they will fight for American families and the issues they care about, like raising incomes, ensuring equal pay for equal work, and making college affordable—policies that will help all Americans get ahead and stay ahead.

The GOP has become more extreme, intolerant, and conservative than ever before. The Party is not able to bring people together, and they certainly will not be able to win elections. That is why swing and independent voters are flocking to the Democrats—because they are turned off by a Party that divides the country and panders to ideological extremism. Donald Trump has a net minus 27 favorability rating among Independent general election voters,[6] and loses to Hillary by 9 points among swing voters in a general election matchup.[7] Hillary enjoys much stronger support among her own Party than Trump does among the GOP, and about a quarter of Republicans say they will defect to the Democratic Party with Trump as the nominee.[8] Hillary is able to build a coalition of support that she will also use once she is in the White House to get things done for America.

The new American electorate represents the future, and so does Hillary. While the GOP wants to bring this country backward, with economic policies that favor the wealthy over American families, and social policies that discriminate and deny Americans equality under the law, Hillary and other Democrats will bring this country forward, and build a strong America where all Americans have the opportunity to thrive.

# 42 ▶ She's a Mother and a Grandmother

*"Maybe it's the grandmother in me, but I believe that part of public service is planting trees under whose shade you'll never sit."*
— Hillary Clinton[1]

*"I won the Mom jackpot . . . and I didn't know that I could love and admire and respect my mom any more, until I became a mom. And [I] couldn't believe any more in her as the right leader for the country I want my daughter to grow up in."*
— Chelsea Clinton[2]

Everyone knows that being a mother is one of the hardest jobs in the world. Raising children to be healthy, contributing members of society is one of the greatest gifts a mother can give to her country. Beyond developing a compassion and patience that only mothers can have for their children, mothers are also some of the best multi-taskers around—need a 100-page legal brief done, a full dinner on the table, and a clean house, all in one day? Just ask a mother to get it done, and she will. Perhaps more than anything, mothers develop a pragmatism that our country needs more of. Hillary considers her job as a mother to be her most cherished accomplishment in life,[3] and her experience as a mother will greatly benefit the United States, an accomplishment that will be a first for a US president.

Hillary's experience as a *working* mother has led to her commitment to fighting for moms and working families. When Hillary was pregnant with Chelsea, the law firm where she worked didn't offer a maternity policy, and many of her colleagues questioned whether Hillary should be allowed to take time off to care for her newborn. When Hillary eventually came back to work, the partners at her law firm made it clear they thought it was shameful for her to leave her baby at home and choose to come back to work.[4] Even though Hillary was fortunate enough to get the time off she needed to be with Chelsea, the judgment she received from her colleagues stayed with her, and underscores the frustration that many working moms feel—today, a quarter of all women in America have to leave their newborn and return to work within ten days of giving birth because they have no paid leave.[5] That's why Hillary wants to support working moms by guaranteeing paid family leave, making child care more affordable, and raising the minimum wage—all of which are critical to Hillary's plan for strengthening American families.[6]

Moms know how important it is to equip our children with the tools they need to build their own successful, happy lives. For Hillary, that starts with early childhood education. She has spent her career working to provide children with the opportunities they need to live up to their God-given potential. In 2007, as senator, Hillary introduced a national initiative to provide funding to states to establish high-quality pre-K programs, including providing free pre-K to children from low-income homes. As president, Hillary will invest in early childhood education programs like Early Head Start. She also has a proposal that would ensure every four year old in America has access to high-quality preschool in the next ten years.[7]

Not only is Hillary a mother, but she is now a grandmother. Hillary has credited her granddaughter Charlotte as her inspiration in running for president, citing concern about the world in which Charlotte will grow up: "Becoming a grandmother has made me think deeply about the responsibility we all share as stewards of the world we inherit and will one day pass on. Rather than make me want to slow down, it has spurred me to speed up."[8] Indeed, Hillary has said on countless occasions that one of the primary goals of her presidency will be to ensure that every child in America has the same opportunities that Charlotte will have, in education, healthcare, and the workplace.[9]

While Hillary is arguably one of the strongest, toughest women in American politics, her experiences as a mother and a grandmother show a softer, more compassionate side that she will bring to her policies—and politics—as president. Hillary cares about American families, especially moms, because she is one, and she knows how important it is for our country to ensure moms and American families can succeed.

# 43 ▶ She Knows the World

*"I could sit in my office and do videoconferences nearly anywhere in the world, but because that is so easy, people actually expect you to show up more, to make the effort and demonstrate the respect, to sit across the table and look eye to eye. It reflects a commitment to the relationship that you cannot get from sending an e-mail or doing a videoconference."*

—Hillary Clinton[1]

Hillary is arguably the most traveled presidential candidate the United States has ever seen—during her tenure as secretary of state, she visited 112 different countries,[2] traveling a total of nearly 1 million miles around the world.[3] Many of her visits were to countries that no secretary of state had ever visited before.[4] But more than just racking up frequent flyer miles, Hillary's travels were part of her strategy to invest time and energy into personal relationships, listening to leaders across the globe, and gaining a real understanding of each country's political situation. Hillary's experience building these relationships around the world will be critical to her foreign policy as president, which will prioritize coming together with other world leaders to form coalitions and solve problems.

One critical trip Hillary took was in November of 2012, to Jerusalem and Cairo, where she met with Israeli Prime Minister Benjamin Netanyahu, Palestinian President Mahmoud Abbas, and Egyptian President Mohamed Morsi. Hillary was able to negotiate a ceasefire between Israel and Hamas, ending the severe turmoil in the Gaza Strip.[5] Hillary's sense that personal investment of time was needed to accomplish this goal reflects her ability to build strategic relationships to get things done.

But beyond the specific conflicts Hillary helped solve, her ability to build relationships with world leaders also helped restore America's reputation around the world. After the Bush Administration and the unpopular wars fought in the Middle East, America's credibility was badly damaged. Hillary was able to improve America's reputation through her development of key relationships as well as her use of smart power—coupling diplomacy with the threat of force or sanctions. As Clinton tells it:

> *The most important thing I did was to help restore America's leadership in the world. And I think that was a very important accomplishment. We were flat on our back when I walked in there the first time. We were viewed as being untrustworthy, as violating our moral rules and values, as being economically hobbled. And we had to get out there and once again promote American values and pursue our interests and protect national security. Because of the eight years that preceded us— it was the economic collapse, it was two wars, it was the war on terror that led to some very unfortunate, un-American actions being taken. That was my biggest challenge. It was why the president asked me to be secretary of state.*[6]

Hillary's willingness to invest time and energy to build personal relationships to reach common goals will aid her greatly as president, where relationships, compromise, and negotiation are the building blocks for success. Her presidency will symbolize strength and respect, while Republicans like Donald Trump would be not only an embarrassment to our country, but a legitimate threat if leaders of other countries are unwilling to work with him, as some have suggested.[7] Hillary's solid relationships with world leaders will enable her to get things done that will benefit the American people.

 **She's Badass**

*"In my White House, we will know who wears the pantsuits."*
—Hillary Clinton[1]

While Hillary is sometimes accused of seeming too scripted and cautious, those who really know her have a very different impression. Those close to Hillary say that she is actually a blast to be around. Governor McAuliffe of Virginia, and Hillary's former campaign chair, said this about Secretary Clinton: "When I'm ready for a cold beer, I don't go looking for Bill Clinton. I go looking for Hillary Clinton. Because she's a lot more fun than Bill Clinton is!"[2] Hillary's showcasing of her dance moves—her whips and nae naes—on a fall 2015 episode of the *Ellen DeGeneres Show* provides additional evidence that Hillary knows how to have a good time.[3]

But Hillary is more than just fun to hang with, she's a total badass. Here's some evidence to support that:

- She rocks her pantsuits: Hillary is not just known for wearing pantsuits, but also for totally rocking them. She regularly features the different colors and styles on her Instagram page.[4]
- She puts Tabasco sauce on everything: Hillary considers Tabasco sauce and red pepper flakes to be among the "basics" that she packs whenever she goes anywhere.[5]
- She wears sunglasses indoors: The famous picture of Hillary chilling on a jet, Blackberry in hand, and sunglasses on, spawned the now-famous meme "Texts From Hillary."[6] She was also spotted ordering food at Chipotle recently, while wearing sunglasses indoors, a combination that makes her extra badass.[7]
- She's just the right amount of hipster: Her campaign headquarters are located in Brooklyn, NY. She also held a fundraiser

at Brooklyn Bowl which is located in Williamsburg, the capital of all hipsters.[8]
- She's not basic: Hillary's not a fan of Pumpkin Spice Lattes.[9]
- She's not afraid to make controversial statements: See bullet immediately above.
- She's a grandmother: Hillary makes being a grandma cool. She's going to make the hashtag #GrandmotherInChief trend.

Her dry humor and witty quips are the hallmark of Hillary's badassness, as the following quotes demonstrate:

- On sexism in the media: "If I want to knock a story off the front page, I just change my hairstyle."[10]
- In response to Republican criticism that she's playing the gender card: "There is a gender card being played in this campaign. It's played every time Republicans vote against giving women equal pay, deny families access to affordable child care or family leave, refuse to let women make decisions about their health or have access to free contraception. These aren't just women's issues, they are economic issues that drive growth and affect all Americans."[11]
- When asked what Bill thinks of her foreign policy decisions: "You want me to tell you what my husband thinks? My husband is not secretary of state; I am. If you want my opinion, I will tell you my opinion. I am not going to be channeling my husband."[12]
- On criticizing the Bush Administration: "I'm sick and tired of people who say that if you debate and disagree with this administration, somehow you're not patriotic. We need to stand up and say we're Americans, and we have the right to debate and disagree with any administration."[13]
- On never giving up: "I think by now people know: I don't quit."[14]
- On not being a good politician: "I am not a natural politician,

in case you haven't noticed, like my husband or President Obama. So I have a view that I just have to do the best I can, get the results I can, make a difference in people's lives, and hope people see that I am fighting for them."[15]

In all seriousness, Hillary is a badass because she's fearless, tough as nails, and committed to getting the job done. And that's what our country needs—a leader who is not afraid to stand up for what's right and for the good of our country. And she might just have fun dancing and looking good in her pantsuits while doing it!

# 45 ► She's a Midwesterner

*"I am the granddaughter of a factory worker. I grew up in the Midwest. Born in Chicago, raised outside of that great city. I was raised with Midwestern values and an unshakeable faith in America and its promise."*
—Hillary Clinton[1]

Unbeknownst to many, Hillary was born and raised in the Midwest, in suburban Illinois, with her parents and two brothers.[2] Both her parents came from humble roots, especially her mother who was abandoned as a child and started working at the age of fourteen to support herself.[3] Hillary's father, the son of a factory laborer, fought for our country in World War II and then returned to civilian life and became a small business owner.[4] It was through her family and Midwestern community that Hillary developed the smart pragmatism that has led to her success as a political leader—she is a progressive who gets things done, and at a time when Washington seems paralyzed by never-ending gridlock, Hillary's Midwestern no-nonsense approach to solving problems is exactly what America needs.

Growing up in the Midwest, Hillary learned the values that made America so great: hard work, perseverance, community, and responsibility. Her mother, Dorothy Rodham, learned early in life the value of personal responsibility—discarded as a young child by her birth parents, she was sent to live with relatives who shunned her, and was then forced to work to support herself as a young girl. Despite these circumstances, Hillary's mother never gave up, and eventually made a life for herself. Dorothy instilled the value of perseverance in her children, often repeating to Hillary that "Life's not about what happens to you, it's about what you do with what happens to you—so get back out there."[5]

It was also in the Midwest that Hillary learned the value of hard work. Her grandfather was a factory worker who labored tirelessly for fifty years in a lace mill. Hillary's father scrimped and saved his money so he could start his own business printing drapery fabric.[6] Both Hillary's grandfather and father believed in the American Dream—that hard work will pay off, and that every American can have the opportunity to get ahead.

Hillary is running for president to restore the basic bargain that her grandparents and parents believed in—that if you do your part and work hard, you and your family should be able to get ahead and stay ahead. But the ideal that any American can achieve success through hard work has fallen by the wayside, as rampant income and wealth inequality plague our country. Americans are working harder than ever before—in the past four decades, worker productivity has increased by 72 percent, but wages have remained almost stagnant, growing only 9 percent.[7] Corporate CEOs and executives reap the benefits of increased productivity and profits while American families struggle. Hillary wants to change this equation so that hard work and perseverance once again mean that American families can have the chance to build a good life.

Hillary's plan to build a strong, fair economy starts with raising the minimum wage for American workers. She also wants to incentivize companies that share their profits with employees.[8] The daughter of a small business owner, Hillary knows that small businesses are the engine of the economy, and has developed plans to support them by expanding access to capital, providing tax relief, cutting red tape, and helping small business owners bring their goods to new markets.[9]

Perhaps most importantly, it is the Midwestern value of perseverance—never giving up—that she learned from her mother that will make Hillary a great president.[10] Hillary has endured much in her political career—from the Lewinsky scandal, to her devastating loss to Barack Obama in 2008, to the grueling eleven-hour Republican-led interrogation on Benghazi. Hillary has been criticized, scrutinized, and knocked down arguably more than any politician in America, let alone any woman politician, yet she always gets right back up and never stops trying. As Hillary herself says, "I think you know by now that I've been called many things by many people—'quitter' is not one of them."[11] And that's what America needs—a champion, a fighter for American families who will never give up on us.

# 46 ▶ She Turned Bill Down (At First)

*"I was terrified about losing my identity and getting lost in the wake of Bill's force-of-nature personality. I actually turned him down twice when he asked me to marry him."*

—Hillary Clinton[1]

Hillary's early relationship with Bill Clinton exemplifies some of her best personality traits—her strength, her independence, and most of all, her commitment to making tough choices. Hillary and Bill met at Yale Law School and were in the library when Hillary, sitting with some of her friends, noticed a man across the way staring at her. This went on for some time before Hillary stood up, marched over to Bill, and said: "You know, if you're going to keep looking at me, and I'm going to keep looking back, we should know each other. I'm Hillary Rodham."[2] Her assertiveness and confidence impressed Bill, who said of his wife, "She conveyed a sense of strength and self-possession I had rarely seen in anyone, man or woman."[3]

In the early 1970s, Bill proposed marriage to Hillary twice before she finally accepted. As Hillary describes her ambivalence: "I was desperately in love with him but utterly confused about my life and future . . . so I said 'No not now'—what I meant was 'Give me time.'"[4] Before entering a marriage, Hillary wanted to be sure she was clear and confident about her own future, including her career goals. Her display of independence and desire to build her own future first was trailblazing for a woman in the 1970s—when marriage and children were still thought of as a woman's ultimate goal.[5]

But more than serving as an example for other working women, Hillary's decision to delay marriage also reflects her strong sense of self and unwavering commitment to making smart choices, even when they're tough to make. Not only has Hillary demonstrated this in her personal life, but also in her career. She stood with Planned Parenthood amid the controversy surrounding allegations about the organization's use of fetal tissue. Despite the media circus over the undercover videos and pressure to call for an investigation into the claims, Hillary remained strong in her commitment to Planned Parenthood and against Republicans who want to defund the organization, asserting that "if this feels like a full-on assault on women's health, that's because it is . . . when politicians talk about defunding Planned Parenthood, they're talking about blocking millions of women, men and young people from live-saving preventive care."[6]

Perhaps the most well-known example of Hillary making a hard choice is her decision to stay married to Bill after the Lewinsky scandal. Despite the harsh judgment she received for doing so, Hillary chose to keep her family intact, not only because she loves and respects Bill, but because she believes in forgiveness and second chances.[7] Hillary credits her own mother for inspiring her to move forward from the scandal and channel her energy toward a political career of her own, so she could be more than the jilted First Lady.[8] Whatever the personal reasons for her decision, they ultimately led her to where she is today—one of the most powerful women in America.

Hillary's unwavering commitment to making smart decisions not only for herself, but for the country and the world, will benefit American families who are counting on a leader who isn't afraid to make tough choices.

# 47 ▶ She Admits When She's Wrong

*"I won't get everything right. Lord knows I've made my share of mistakes. Well, there's no shortage of people pointing them out! And I certainly haven't won every battle I've fought. But leadership means perseverance and hard choices. You have to push through the setbacks and disappointments and keep at it."*

—Hillary Clinton[1]

While the decisions Hillary has made in her life and career have led to extraordinary accomplishments and results that have benefitted American families everywhere, she has also made some mistakes along the way. An important leadership quality is the ability to recognize your own shortcomings, and grow from them. As we all know, it's not easy to admit wrongdoing, but it is critical that we do so—both to maintain our personal integrity, and also to learn and do better next time. And that's what Hillary has done—like all human beings, she has made mistakes, and some of them have carried very serious consequences. But each time, Hillary has not only admitted her wrongs, she has grown from her mistakes as well.

In 2002, Hillary voted, along with the vast majority of the Senate, to authorize President Bush's invasion of Iraq.[2] At the time, the Bush Administration justified the Iraq War on the grounds that the country's brutal dictator, Saddam Hussein, was harboring WMDs (Weapons of Mass Destruction)—an assertion that was later found to be false.[3] Meanwhile, thousands of American troops and over a million Iraqis died in a war that destabilized the region and fueled the rise of Islamic extremist groups like ISIS.[4]

Hillary has since declared that her vote for the Iraq War was a mistake. On the campaign trail, she has been very open about her error, telling Iowa voters recently, "I made a mistake, plain and simple . . . What we now see is a very different and very dangerous situation."[5]

Hillary also made a mistake earlier in her career, when she failed to fully embrace the rights of LGBT Americans to marry. During the 2008 campaign, both Hillary and her rival, then-Senator Barack Obama, expressed support for civil unions and domestic partnerships but not same-sex marriage. [6] But like the American public, both President Obama and Hillary shifted in their feelings toward same-sex marriage. As Hillary explained her change of heart: "I think I'm an American. And I think we have all evolved, and it's been one of the fastest, most sweeping transformations."[7] Ensuring that every couple and family can love, live, pray, and work free from discrimination is a priority for Hillary, and she will fight hard for the rights of LGBT individuals and families in America.

During her time as secretary of state, Hillary used a personal email address and private server to conduct official state business.[8] Because some of the emails may have contained sensitive information, many were concerned that Hillary's actions could have posed a threat to security.[9] After explaining that use of a private server did not violate State Department protocols or procedures in any way, Hillary apologized for her actions and expressed regret: "As I look back at it now, even though it was allowed, I should have used two accounts. That was a mistake. I'm sorry about that. I take responsibility."[10] It was later revealed that former secretaries of state, including Republican Colin Powell, had also used private email addresses to conduct business.[11]

Mistakes are a part of the human condition—everyone makes them, and no one is perfect. It is what you do after the mistake that really matters. Hillary is willing to take responsibility for her mistakes, while her Republican opponents adamantly refuse to consider that they made the wrong decision—about Iraq, same-sex marriage, and a host of other policies that have harmed American families.[12] Americans deserve a leader who can be honest in admitting errors in judgment and not shift the blame elsewhere. Hillary has shown that she can not only recognize the error of her ways, but she can move forward from them, and make better decisions in the future. Her thoughtful, conscientious leadership will set an example of responsibility and accountability for the American people.

# 48 ► She Is the Most Admired Woman in America

*"I've known Hillary for over thirty years. I've watched her growth. I've admired her from a distance. She's a leader. She's fearless in speaking out. And I watched her as First Lady, Senator, Secretary of State. I think there's never been anybody quite so experienced and capable who would stand for the Office of President of the United States."*
—General Wesley Clark[1]

Hillary has been voted the "Most Admired Woman in America" in national polls of American adults a record twenty times, including this past year.[2] Americans admire Hillary for her experience and accomplishments and because she never gives up—on herself or the Americans she is fighting for.

Hillary has earned the respect of leaders around the world, who also admire her experience and tenacity. As secretary of state, she was widely credited with restoring America's reputation in the eyes of the world.[3] Her accomplishments have been lauded by Democrats and Republicans alike—John McCain said of Hillary: "I admire the fact that she is admired throughout the world and a very effective secretary of state."[4] And former Secretary of State Henry Kissinger, also a Republican, said Hillary "ran the State Department in the most effective way that I've ever seen."[5]

In addition to commanding the respect and admiration of world leaders and the American public, Hillary has also won the admiration of children, including young girls who see Hillary as a role model.[6] Despite the enormous barriers Hillary has faced as a woman in the historically male-dominated world of politics, she has broken every one of those barriers down, and in the process has set an example for girls and women everywhere. As one little girl said in a letter she wrote to Hillary, "You inspire me so that I can be who I want to be when I grow up."[7]

Hillary's accomplishments did not come easy, as she has spent decades weathering scrutiny, criticism, and attacks of the worst kind. Despite Hillary's devastating loss to Barack Obama in 2008, she is running for president again because she believes in America's future, and wants to continue the work she has spent her life doing—ensuring that all Americans have a fair shot in life. She wants to continue breaking down barriers so that all Americans—regardless of gender, race, country of origin, or sexual orientation—can pursue their dreams. The American people admire Hillary's tenacity, and they know that she will bring this fighting spirit to the White House, where she will never give up on the American people.

# 49 ▶ She Can Work with Republicans

*"I'd like to bring people from the right, left, red, blue, get them into a nice, warm purple space where everybody is talking and where we're actually trying to solve problems."*

—Hillary Clinton[1]

Hillary Clinton is a progressive who knows how to get things done.[2] She understands that solving problems often requires reaching across the aisle and working with Republicans toward common sense solutions that benefit American families. In a political environment that suffers from gridlock, divisiveness, and polarization, Hillary's no-nonsense approach and ability to bring people together to deliver results will be a welcome change.

Hillary learned how to work with the GOP early in life when she herself was an active young Republican who supported Barry Goldwater in 1964. The daughter of a "rock-ribbed, up-by-your-bootstraps conservative Republican" father (and a Democratic mother),[3] Hillary grew up in the Midwest, where conservative values triumphed. But after Hillary was given an assignment in school to research President Johnson's positions for a mock debate, Hillary began to move to the left, and by 1968 she supported Democrat Eugene McCarthy for president.[4] Hillary's upbringing and short stint as a Republican ultimately helped her in her career, because she is in touch with Republicans and conservative values in a way that someone who grew up among liberals in the Northeast or West all their lives simply could not be. Far from making Hillary a flip flopper, this experience has enabled her to speak the language of conservatives and successfully reach across the aisle to build solutions.

Hillary's record demonstrates her strong commitment to bipartisan solutions. In the Senate, she teamed up with Senator James Inhofe (R–OK), notorious for his denial of climate change, on utilizing geothermal energy to power federal buildings as a way of reducing costs and improving energy efficiency. Together they ensured the provision would be included in a comprehensive energy bill.[5]

On behalf of veterans, Hillary joined Senator Jeff Sessions (R–AL), one of the staunchest conservatives in Congress, in introducing a bill guaranteeing full payment of bonuses to wounded veterans.[6] The bill passed the Senate with unanimous consent.[7]

In both examples, Hillary reached across the aisle in the name of a greater good—cleaner energy and support for our veterans. She did the same thing as secretary of state, working with Republicans to guarantee the health and security of the United States. Republicans have praised her performance, and even some of her biggest rivals admit her effectiveness, including Jeb Bush, who said of Hillary: "Hillary and I come from different political parties and we disagree about lots of things. But we do agree on the wisdom of the American people."[8] Senator Lindsey Graham, (R–SC), said this in praise of the secretary: "I think she's represented our nation well. She is extremely well respected throughout the world, handles herself in a very classy way and has a work ethic second to none."[9]

With a lifetime in public service, Hillary has longstanding relationships with both Democrat and Republican lawmakers, as well as the policy expertise, political savviness, and leadership skills she has developed through her experience. Although some of Hillary's opponents have touted their "outsider" status, it is Hillary's knowledge, clout, and ability to forge consensus that will make her an effective president. While some believe her experience is a liability in an election that seems to favor non-traditional candidates, her background is an extraordinary asset that will serve the American people and ensure our country can move toward common sense solutions that work for American families. In fact, her ability to get things done in a system that seems frozen in gridlock is about as anti-establishment as you can get!

# 50 ▶ She Knows How to Negotiate

*"I'm a progressive that likes to get things done."*

—Hillary Clinton[1]

In the political world, Hillary is one of the best negotiators there is. She knows that successful negotiations rely not on coercion or brute force, but on relationship-building, compromise, and respect. As secretary of state, Hillary made deals that elevated America's position in the world and kept Americans safe. As president, she will use her negotiation skills not only in world affairs, but right here at home to make sure Congress and the rest of government get things done for the American people.

Hillary Clinton's effectiveness as secretary of state has been widely praised. Her accomplishments are owed in part to her superb negotiating skills and ability to make deals that benefit the United States. For example, one of Hillary's greatest accomplishments is negotiating the ceasefire between Hamas and Israel.[2] Through Hillary's work bringing Hamas to the negotiating table, she was able to end rocket attacks and airstrikes that had killed nearly 200 people. Hillary's negotiations also averted an Israeli invasion of the Gaza Strip, which would have caused casualties to skyrocket.[3] Hillary's negotiating skills made this deal possible.

Also as secretary of state, Hillary forged an international coalition to sanction Iran and keep them at the negotiating table to strike a nuclear agreement. Hillary convinced all 27 nations in the European Union to stop importing Iranian oil and all 20 major global importers of Iranian oil—including Japan, India, China, and Turkey—to make significant cuts that crippled Iran's economy.[4] Her negotiations were essential in bringing Iran to the table and ultimately led to the nuclear deal.

As president, Hillary will continue to use her expert negotiating skills to keep our country safe. She will vigorously enforce the Iran deal and will not hesitate to impose sanctions or military action if necessary should Iran be found shirking its obligations.[5] She will also include women, who can be great agents of peace and change, at the negotiating table.[6] Hillary made many efforts as secretary of state to include women as part of security and peacemaking strategies and will build on this important work as president.[7]

Hillary will also negotiate with Republicans to get things done for the American people. She's done this throughout her career, including in the Senate when she teamed up with Republican senators to pass a clean energy bill[8] and guarantee benefits for wounded veterans.[9] Hillary has decades of experience bringing people together to solve problems, and that is exactly what she will do as president.

Hillary is a practical progressive who gets things done. She values consensus and compromise, not the bullying and force that Republicans like Donald Trump advocate. Her exceptional negotiating skills have led to big wins for America, and she will continue her record of negotiating on behalf of the American people so that our country can move forward to a brighter future.

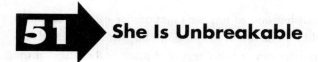

# 51 ▶ She Is Unbreakable

*"I'd come home from a hard day at the Senate or the State Department, sit down with [my mother] at the small table in our breakfast nook, and just let everything pour out. And she would remind me why we keep fighting, even when the odds are long and the opposition is fierce. I can still hear her saying: 'Life's not about what happens to you, it's about what you do with what happens to you—so get back out there.'"*

—Hillary Clinton, on her mother[1]

Hillary is a fighter, and it's in her blood. Dorothy Rodham, Hillary's mother, came from a broken home and was abandoned by her parents at a young age. She briefly lived with her grandparents until she left to live on her own at the age of 14, working as a housekeeper for $3 a week. Despite her difficult childhood, Dorothy overcame great odds and thrived. Her remarkable resilience, coupled with her determination to keep fighting and never give up, had a profound effect on Hillary. Indeed, Hillary herself says of her mother, "No one had a bigger influence on my life or did more to shape the person I became."[2]

A look at Hillary's history reveals her tremendous strength and tenacity—at once, she is the most admired and the most criticized woman in America. She has survived decades of intense scrutiny and the pressure of being in the public spotlight, including a devastating loss to Barack Obama during the 2008 Democratic primary. But even after her loss, she put aside rivalry for the benefit of her Party and endorsed Obama, and eventually joined his Cabinet as secretary of state.

And who could forget the Lewinsky scandal, a very public humiliation for Hillary and her family, which eventually led to her husband's impeachment. Looking back at that devastating moment in her life, Hillary credits her mother for pushing her to move beyond the infamy and launch her own political career, to be known for being more than just the jilted First Lady.[3]

More recently, Hillary demonstrated her tremendous strength and ability to withstand scrutiny during the eleven-hour marathon hearing before the Republican Select Committee on Benghazi. Throughout the ordeal, Hillary kept her patience, appeared poised and confident, and answered the pointed, critical, and oftentimes contemptuous questions lobbed her way from Republican members of Congress. Hillary's responses in the hearing were widely praised in the press. A *Slate* article says of Hillary: "Clinton was strong. Throughout, she showed her clear knowledge of foreign policy questions, defended the administration and her tenure at the State Department, and laid out her vision for how American diplomacy should operate."[4] Even Fox News admitted Hillary was "visibly measured" in her responses.[5] Her ability to withstand such pressure while simultaneously appearing poised, composed, and smart is very much befitting of the next leader of the United States of America.

In the 2016 primaries, she encountered enormous criticism in an election year when "outsider" candidates were favored. But when her opponents tried to frame Hillary's experience as a liability, she reminded voters how a proven record of accomplishments is what sets her apart as a candidate. Hillary is not only a progressive, but a progressive who gets things done.

If that's not enough to convince you Hillary is unbreakable, she also beat John McCain in a drinking contest—with vodka, no less![6]

Like her mother, Hillary is unbreakable. No matter how big the loss or how painful the ordeal, Hillary never gives up. Governor of Virginia Terry McAuliffe has praised Hillary's tenacity: "She's been beaten up, she's been knocked down, but every time she does, she gets right back up. She dusts herself off, and she gets right back in that arena again."[7] And what that means for our country is profound—it means that Hillary will never stop working for everyday Americans, she will "be a champion for American families of all kinds, from one end of our country to the next, to make sure that every single person has a chance to live up to his or her God-given potential."[8] A strong country starts with a strong leader, and that leader is Hillary.

# 52 She Will Make America Whole

*"Despite what you hear, we don't need to make America great again: America has never stopped being great. But we do need to make America whole again. Instead of building walls, we need to be tearing down barriers. We need to show by everything we do that we really are in this together."*

—Hillary Clinton[1]

America has always been a great country—we are a nation of some of the best innovators, problem-solvers, and leaders this world has ever seen. Our values—freedom, fairness, opportunity, and respect for human dignity—are what have drawn so many to our shores, and are what inspire people across the globe. At times we have fallen short of living up to those values, because in many ways our country has been divided for too long—along lines of race, ethnicity, socioeconomic status, and ideology. The most critical mission of the next leader of the free world is to bring Americans together to solve some of the most pressing issues of our time and make America whole again. This is a task that Hillary Clinton is ready and willing to do on day one. She knows that America has always been great, but to move forward into the future and become the nation we want to be, the nation we want our children and grandchildren to inherit, we need to make America whole.

The tone and tenor of this campaign have already made clear that Donald Trump and other Republicans will do the opposite of making America whole—they will divide and polarize the country even more, in a shallow and desperate attempt to leverage the dark side of the American psyche to gain political advantage. Their message is one of anger, intolerance, and hatred. Donald Trump has degraded almost every group in this country, denying the humanity of immigrants, people of color, LGBT people, war veterans, and women.[2] Republicans want to roll back the great gains and progress we have made as Americans. Sadly, the GOP today represents the Party of the past.

Hillary will be the president of the future and will lead America to becoming the nation we want to be in the twenty-first century. Rather than put up walls, she is going to knock down barriers for all Americans so everyone has a fair shot in life, and everyone has the opportunity to live up to their potential.

Republicans want to build an economy of yesterday, when Wall Street and corporations wrote the rules. Hillary wants to build the economy of tomorrow—where American families can get ahead and stay ahead. Her number one priority as president is to raise incomes for middle-class Americans.[3] She will reject the tried and failed trickle-down economic policies promoted by Republicans and create an economy that is both fair and inclusive. As Hillary says of Republicans: "Fundamentally, they reject what it takes to build an inclusive economy. It takes an inclusive society. What I once called 'a village' that has a place for everyone."[4]

Republicans, however, want to take the country backward across the board—and not just on economic issues. They want to take away health insurance from more than 16 million Americans without offering any credible alternative.[5] They want to take away the right of women to make their own reproductive health choices. They oppose laws that would allow LGBT Americans to live, work, pray, and love, free from discrimination.[6] They deride and insult the humanity of immigrants. And they want to destroy the Social Security and Medicare trust funds that our seniors have spent their lives paying into.[7]

Hillary has a different vision for our country, one that is built on the values of opportunity, fairness, freedom, and respect for human dignity. Hillary's America will be one where every American has an equal chance to succeed in our great country; where the economy works for American families—not just billionaires and CEOs; where all Americans can live their lives without fear of discrimination, gun violence, or a terrorist attack; and where women, LGBT individuals, immigrants, and people of color are afforded the respect they deserve.

This is the country of the future, and Hillary will be the leader who takes us there.

A pragmatic progressive, Hillary has spent her entire life bringing people together, finding compromise, forming coalitions, and getting things done. She knows what it takes to bring America together where we are most fragmented, shattered, and divided. She will make America stronger and stitch us whole again, setting us on the right path for tomorrow.

# NOTES

## I. Opportunity

### 1. She Is Looking Toward the Future, Not the Past

[1] http://blogs.wsj.com/washwire/2015/07/13/hillary-clinton-transcript-building-the-growth-and-fairness-economy/
[2] http://www.usnews.com/opinion/economic-intelligence/2015/08/06/republican-2016-candidates-cling-to-failed-trickle-down-economics-theory
[3] http://time.com/3920332/transcript-full-text-hillary-clinton-campaign-launch/

### 2. She Is a Woman

[1] http://www.crisisgroup.org/en/support/event-calendar/past-events/annual-award-dinner/award-dinner-2011/keynote-address-us-secretary-of-state-hillary-rodham-clinton.aspx
[2] http://www.sciencedirect.com/science/article/pii/S0022103113000206
[3] http://www.huffingtonpost.com/brittany-l-stalsburg-phd/hillary-clinton-support-er_1_b_9266284.html
[4] http://www.bls.gov/news.release/pdf/atus.pdf
[5] http://www.hhs.gov/healthcare/facts/blog/2013/08/womens-health-needs.html
[6] http://www.iwpr.org/initiatives/poverty
[7] https://rainn.org/get-information/statistics/sexual-assault-victims
[8] http://www.politicalparity.org/why-women/
[9] http://www.nytimes.com/2013/10/15/us/senate-women-lead-in-effort-to-find-accord.html?_r=0
[10] http://swampland.time.com/2013/10/16/women-are-the-only-adults-left-in-washington/
[11] http://www.press.uchicago.edu/ucp/books/book/chicago/W/bo15233103.html
[12] http://swampland.time.com/2013/10/16/women-are-the-only-adults-left-in-washington/

### 3. She Will Create Jobs and Rebuild Our Infrastructure

[1] https://medium.com/@HillaryClinton/why-i-oppose-keystone-xl-8698230df2a8
[2] http://www.politico.com/magazine/story/2015/09/carly-fiorina-debate-hillary-clintons-greatest-accomplishment-213157
[3] http://www.streetsblog.org/2008/08/04/hillary-clinton-introduces-senate-version-of-transit-relief-bill/
[4] http://www.theatlantic.com/politics/archive/2015/12/hillary-clintons-modest-infrastructure-proposal/418068/
[5] https://www.hillaryclinton.com/issues/infrastructure/
[6] http://www.brookings.edu/blogs/the-avenue/posts/2016/01/13-flint-water-crisis-infrastructure-kane-puentes

[7] http://www.cnsnews.com/news/article/melanie-hunter/hillary-clinton-it-raining-lead-flint

[8] https://www.hillaryclinton.com/briefing/factsheets/2015/11/30/clinton-infrastructure-plan-builds-tomorrows-economy-today/

[9] http://www.dailykos.com/story/2015/5/15/1383149/-Why-do-Republicans-really-oppose-infrastructure-spending

## 4. She Will Strengthen Our Communities

[1] https://twitter.com/hillaryclinton/status/588078803664113665

[2] http://thehill.com/blogs/ballot-box/presidential-races/204772-group-touts-hillary-clintons-minimum-wage-efforts

[3] https://www.washingtonpost.com/news/post-politics/wp/2016/01/29/equal-pay-litigant-lilly-ledbetter-endorses-clinton/

[4] http://blogs.wsj.com/washwire/2013/12/31/hillary-clinton-calls-for-restoring-job-less-benefits/

[5] https://www.congress.gov/bill/107th-congress/senate-bill/989/cosponsors;

[6] http://web.archive.org/web/20080528220552/http:/www.hillaryclinton.com/news/speech/view/?id=2645

[7] https://www.hillaryclinton.com/briefing/h/2016-02-12-hillary-clintons-breaking-every-barrier-agenda-revitalizing-the-economy-in-communities-left-behind/

[8] http://www.nbcnews.com/news/nbcblk/hillary-clinton-targets-hbcus-college-affordability-plan-n410591

[9] http://web.archive.org/web/20080529023640/http:/www.hillaryclinton.com/news/release/view/?id=7033

[10] http://www.nbcnews.com/news/latino/clinton-sanders-tangle-over-immigration-debate-n535651

[11] http://www.cnn.com/2015/07/15/politics/hillary-clinton-immigration/

## 5. She Will Protect the Environment for Future Generations

[1] http://www.msnbc.com/msnbc/hillary-clinton-goes-green#54979

[2] https://www.govtrack.us/congress/bills/110/s309

[3] http://www.epw.senate.gov/pressitem.cfm?party=dem&id=230866

[4] http://www.state.gov/r/pa/prs/ps/2012/02/184055.htm

[5] http://www.nationaljournal.com/energy/why-environmentalists-are-anxious-about-a-hillary-clinton-2016-run-20150410

[6] https://www.washingtonpost.com/blogs/plum-line/wp/2014/12/04/this-one-hillary-quote-about-climate-change-is-very-very-important/

[7] http://www.theguardian.com/environment/2015/sep/24/hillary-clinton-unveils-her-masterplan-to-make-us-clean-energy-superpower

[8] http://thetoggle.com/hillary-clinton-challenges-renewable-energy-initiatives-with-ambitious-solar-goals/

[9] http://www.detroitnews.com/story/news/michigan/flint-water-crisis/2016/01/29/clinton/79522360/

[10] http://www.detroitnews.com/story/news/michigan/flint-water-crisis/2016/01/29/clinton/79522360/

[11] http://www.theguardian.com/environment/climate-consensus-97-per-cent/2015/oct/05/the-republican-party-stands-alone-in-climate-denial

## 6. She Gets Work/Life Balance

[1] http://www.huffingtonpost.com/2015/05/11/hillary-clinton-paid-family-leave-mothers-day_n_7257370.html

[2] http://abcnews.go.com/US/story?id=93604&page=1

[3] http://makeitworkcampaign.org/issues/work-and-family/

[4] http://www.nationalpartnership.org/issues/work-family/paid-sick-days.html?referrer=https://www.google.com/

[5] http://www.nationalpartnership.org/research-library/work-family/psd/working-women-need-paid-sick-days.pdf

[6] https://www.hillaryclinton.com/issues/womens-rights-and-opportunity/

[7] http://www.presidency.ucsb.edu/ws/?pid=770610

[8] http://www.washingtonpost.com/news/the-fix/wp/2015/07/23/how-hillary-clinton-is-making-the-economic-issues-womens-issues-argument/

[9] http://www.cato.org/publications/cato-online-forum/grow-our-economy-start-paid-leave

[10] http://makeitworkcampaign.org/wp-content/uploads/2015/02/MIW-SOTU-Poll-Memo.pdf

## 7. She Will Advocate for Millennials

[1] http://www.cnn.com/2016/02/03/politics/democratic-town-hall-transcript/

[2] https://www.congress.gov/congressional-record/2006/05/26/senate-section/article/S5344-1

[3] https://www.congress.gov/congressional-record/2006/05/26/senate-section/article/S5344-1

[4] http://thecaucus.blogs.nytimes.com/2007/11/24/clinton-takes-on-student-loan-industry/?_r=0

[5] http://web.archive.org/web/20081218183900/http:/clinton.senate.gov/news/statements/details.cfm?id=302370&&

[6] http://www.nytimes.com/2015/08/10/us/politics/hillary-clinton-to-offer-plan-on-paying-college-tuition-without-needing-loans.html?_r=0

[7] https://www.hillaryclinton.com/issues/college/

[8] http://www.cnn.com/2015/08/10/politics/hillary-clinton-college-affordability/

[9] https://www.hillaryclinton.com/p/briefing/factsheets/2015/08/10/college-compact/

[10] https://www.hillaryclinton.com/p/briefing/factsheets/2015/08/10/college-compact-costs/

[11] http://www.nytimes.com/2015/08/10/us/politics/hillary-clinton-to-offer-plan-on-paying-college-tuition-without-needing-loans.html?_r=0

[12] http://www.msnbc.com/msnbc/planned-parenthood-endorses-hillary-clinton-primary

[13] https://www.hillaryclinton.com/issues/womens-rights-and-opportunity/

[14] http://www.huffingtonpost.com/entry/hillary-clinton-equality-act_55b12877e4b08f57d5d3ed54

[15] http://www.huffingtonpost.com/entry/hillary-clinton-equality-act_55b12877e4b08f57d5d3ed54

[16] http://www.cnn.com/2015/11/22/politics/hillary-clinton-tax-break-caregivers/

[17] http://www.cnn.com/2015/11/22/politics/hillary-clinton-tax-break-caregivers/

## 8. She Will Make Child Care a Priority

[1] http://www.chicagotribune.com/news/local/politics/ct-hillary-clinton-chicago-met-0521-20150521-story.html
[2] http://www.pbs.org/newshour/making-sense/cheaper-parents-stay-home-pay-child-care/
[3] http://web.archive.org/web/20080920065734/http:/www.hillaryclinton.com/news/release/view/?id=6246
[4] http://www.thune.senate.gov/public/index.cfm/press-releases?ID=c1067d23-035c-45a8-954b-959200a8a6cc
[5] https://www.hillaryclinton.com/the-briefing/fact-sheet-equal-pay/
[6] https://www.congress.gov/bill/109th-congress/senate-bill/1085/cosponsors
[7] http://www.cnn.com/2015/08/14/politics/hillary-clinton-scholarship-proposal-iowa/
[8] http://www.huffingtonpost.com/2015/06/15/hillary-clinton-child-care_n_7587024.html

## 9. She Will Invest in Our Children

[1] http://www.cnn.com/2015/09/12/politics/hillary-clinton-charlotte-tv-ad/
[2] Clinton, Hillary Rodham, *It Takes a Village: And Other Lessons Children Teach Us* (New York: Simon & Schuster, 1996).
[3] http://www.childrensdefense.org/newsroom/cdf-in-the-news/press-releases/2013/honoring-hillary-clinton.html?referrer=https://www.google.com/
[4] http://content.time.com/time/magazine/article/0,9171,1722256,00.html
[5] http://kff.org/medicaid/issue-brief/the-impact-of-the-childrens-health-insurance-program-chip-what-does-the-research-tell-us/
[6] https://www.hillaryclinton.com/issues/early-childhood-education/
[7] https://www.hillaryclinton.com/briefing/factsheets/2015/06/14/fact-sheet-universal-preschool/
[8] http://www.washingtonmonthly.com/republic3-0/2016/02/head_start_is_missing_the_popu059715.php
[9] http://www.usnews.com/opinion/knowledge-bank/2015/06/25/why-the-gops-education-funding-bill-gets-an-f

## 10. She Is Committed to Supporting Our Youth

[1] http://www.theguardian.com/us-news/2015/jul/03/hillary-clinton-gay-humans-new-york-teen
[2] http://www.politico.com/magazine/story/2015/04/hillary-clinton-2016-arkansas-116939
[3] http://laprensa-sandiego.org/archieve/august13/white.htm
[4] http://blogs.edweek.org/edweek/campaign-k-12/2015/04/education_and_hillary_clinton_.html
[5] http://www.politico.com/story/2015/10/clinton-nea-teachers-union-endorsement-214402
[6] http://www.washingtonexaminer.com/how-did-the-2016-candidates-vote-on-no-child-left-behind-and-its-replacement/article/2578093

[7] http://www.statista.com/statistics/217448/seasonally-adjusted-monthly-youth-unemployment-rate-in-the-us/

[8] https://www.hillaryclinton.com/briefing/h/2016-02-12-hillary-clintons-breaking-every-barrier-agenda-revitalizing-the-economy-in-communities-left-behind/

[9] http://democrats.budget.house.gov/fact-sheet/fact-sheet-republican-budget-cuts-education

## 11. She Will Expand Space Exploration

[1] http://www.spacepolicyonline.com/news/hillary-clinton-i-really-really-do-support-the-space-program?utm_src=email

[2] http://www.spacepolicyonline.com/news/hillary-clinton-i-really-really-do-support-the-space-program?utm_src=email

[3] http://www.thespacereview.com/article/997/1

[4] http://thehill.com/policy/technology/256580-gop-warns-of-journey-to-nowhere-at-nasa

[5] http://www.spacepolicyonline.com/news/hillary-clinton-i-really-really-do-support-the-space-program

[6] http://www.spacepolicyonline.com/news/hillary-clinton-i-really-really-do-support-the-space-program?utm_src=email

[7] https://www.nasa.gov/mission_pages/newhorizons/overview/index.html

[8] http://www.nasa.gov/press-release/nasa-confirms-evidence-that-liquid-water-flows-on-today-s-mars

## 12. She Will Make Renewable Energy Mainstream

[1] Hillary Clinton, 26 July 2015: http://thetoggle.com/hillary-clinton-challenges-renewable-energy-initiatives-with-ambitious-solar-goals/

[2] http://wwf.panda.org/about_our_earth/aboutcc/cause/

[3] http://climate.nasa.gov/effects/

[4] http://www.epw.senate.gov/pressitem.cfm?party=dem&id=230866

[5] http://www.energy.senate.gov/public/index.cfm/files/serve?File_id=027aaa73-96cf-4570-9075-583e1712c342

[6] http://www.c2es.org/international/negotiations/cop-15/summary

[7] https://www.hillaryclinton.com/issues/climate/

[8] http://www.cnn.com/2015/07/26/politics/clinton-climate-change-renewable-energy/

[9] Hillary_Clinton_Climate_Change_Fact_Sheet%20(3).pdf

[10] http://www.theguardian.com/environment/climate-consensus-97-per-cent/2015/oct/05/the-republican-party-stands-alone-in-climate-denial

[11] http://www.theguardian.com/us-news/video/2015/jul/28/hillary-clinton-unveils-climate-change-policy-video

## 13. She Believes in the American Dream

[1] http://www.bbc.com/news/world-us-canada-33122234

[2] http://www.epi.org/publication/ib330-productivity-vs-compensation/

[3] http://www.realclearmarkets.com/articles/2013/10/01/are_rich_kids_naturally_born_more_able__100639.html

[4] http://www.brookings.edu/blogs/social-mobility-memos/
posts/2015/01/15-mlk-black-opportunity-reeves
[5] http://www.aauw.org/files/2015/09/The-Simple-Truth-Fall-2015.pdf
[6] https://www.congress.gov/bill/110th-congress/senate-bill/2514?q=%7B%22search
%22%3A%5B%22S.2514%22%5D%7D
[7] https://www.govtrack.us/congress/bills/109/s841
[8] https://www.congress.gov/bill/111th-congress/senate-bill/244/cosponsors
[9] https://www.hillaryclinton.com/issues/college/
[10] Ibid.
[11] http://www.msnbc.com/msnbc/hillary-clinton-i-favor-12-hour-minimum-wage
[12] https://www.hillaryclinton.com/p/briefing/factsheets/2015/07/16/profit-sharing/
[13] http://www.newyorker.com/magazine/2015/11/09/the-republican-class-war

## II. Fairness

## 14. She Will Create a Strong and Fair Economy for All Americans

[1] http://www.latimes.com/nation/la-na-hillary-clinton-economy-20150713-story.html
[2] http://www.epi.org/productivity-pay-gap/
[3] http://www.epi.org/productivity-pay-gap/
[4] http://clinton6.nara.gov/1996/08/1996-08-20-president-remarks-on-signing-min-imum-wage-bill.html
[5] https://www.congress.gov/bill/110th-congress/senate-bill/2514?q=%7B%22search
%22%3A%5B%22S.2514%22%5D%7D
[6] https://www.hillaryclinton.com/issues/plan-raise-american-incomes/
[7] https://www.hillaryclinton.com/p/briefing/factsheets/2015/08/10/college-com-pact-costs/
[8] http://www.inc.com/hillary-clinton/four-ways-to-jump-start-small-business.html
[9] https://www.hillaryclinton.com/issues/plan-raise-american-incomes/
[10] http://www.reuters.com/article/2015/07/11/us-usa-election-clinton-tax-idUSKCN0PL0QM20150711
[11] http://www.reuters.com/article/2015/07/16/us-usa-election-clinton-ecolnom-ic-idUSKCN0PQ27N20150716
[12] http://www.epi.org/publication/raising-the-minimum-wage-to-12-by-2020-would-lift-wages-for-35-million-american-workers
[13] http://www.nytimes.com/2015/04/23/business/economy/democrats-are-rallying-around-12-wage-floor.html?_r=0
[14] http://www.epi.org/minimum-wage-statement/
[15] http://ourfinancialsecurity.org/blogs/wp-content/ourfinancialsecurity.org/
uploads/2012/09/CostCrisis2015July-Long.pdf
[16] http://www.thestreet.com/video/13318035/hillary-clinton-calls-for-expansion-of-dodd-frank-high-frequency-trading-tax.html
[17] http://www.usnews.com/opinion/economic-intelligence/2015/08/06/republican-2016-candidates-cling-to-failed-trickle-down-economics-theory
[18] http://www.washingtonpost.com/video/politics/clinton-hits-republicans-on-econ-omy/2015/10/17/01d5a688-7507-11e5-ba14-318f8e87a2fc_video.html
[19] http://www.theamericanconservative.com/2014/01/31/how-the-gop-sold-out-middle-america-for-corporate-america/

## 15. She Will Strengthen Our Democracy

[1] June 4, 2015: https://www.hillaryclinton.com/the-four-fights/revitalizing-our-democracy/

[2] https://www.jstor.org/stable/1350315?seq=1#page_scan_tab_contents; http://www.eac.gov/assets/1/Page/2014_EAC_EAVS_Comprehensive_Report_508_Compliant.pdf

[3] https://www.hillaryclinton.com/the-four-fights/revitalizing-our-democracy/

[4] http://www.washingtonpost.com/politics/hillary-clinton-calls-for-sweeping-expansion-of-voter-registration/2015/06/04/691f210c-0adb-11e5-9e39-0db921c47b93_story.html

[5] https://www.brennancenter.org/analysis/voter-id

[6] http://www.washingtonpost.com/news/wonkblog/wp/2014/07/09/7-papers-4-government-inquiries-2-news-investigations-and-1-court-ruling-proving-voter-fraud-is-mostly-a-myth/

[7] http://www.theguardian.com/us-news/2015/aug/06/hillary-clinton-republicans-voting-rights-restrictions-fearmongering

## 16. She Will Tackle Economic Inequality

[1] http://www.washingtonexaminer.com/hillary-clinton-releases-ad-aimed-at-middle-class/article/2570451

[2] http://www.theguardian.com/business/2014/nov/13/us-wealth-inequality-top-01-worth-as-much-as-the-bottom-90

[3] http://inequality.org/income-inequality/#sthash.NVSVxRSv.dpuf

[4] http://www.huffingtonpost.com/entry/worker-productivity-pay-gap_us_55e741ed-e4b0c818f61a3dee

[5] https://www.congress.gov/bill/109th-congress/senate-bill/2725

[6] https://www.congress.gov/bill/109th-congress/senate-bill/841?q=%7B%22search%22%3A%5B%22Paycheck+Fairness+Act%22%5D%7D

[7] http://www.senate.gov/legislative/LIS/roll_call_lists/roll_call_vote_cfm.cfm?congress=107&session=1&vote=00170

[8] http://www.forbes.com/sites/anthonynitti/2015/04/13/what-hillary-clintons-voting-record-reveals-about-her-tax-plan/2/#3bba47936aae

[9] https://votesmart.org/candidate/key-votes/55463/hillary-clinton/93/higher-education#.VugTXpwrKUk

[10] https://www.hillaryclinton.com/issues/plan-raise-american-incomes/

[11] http://www.huffingtonpost.com/entry/hillary-clinton-12-minimum-wage_55ba7988e4b0b23e3ce1f307

[12] https://www.hillaryclinton.com/p/briefing/factsheets/2015/07/16/profit-sharing/

[13] https://www.hillaryclinton.com/the-briefing/fact-sheet-equal-pay/

[14] http://www.iwpr.org/publications/pubs/how-equal-pay-for-working-women-would-reduce-poverty-and-grow-the-american-economy

[15] https://grabien.com/file.php?id=51664

[16] http://www.nytimes.com/2015/10/17/business/putting-numbers-to-a-tax-increase-for-the-rich.html

[17] http://www.bloomberg.com/politics/articles/2015-11-12/rising-income-inequality-causes-republicans-to-shift-rhetoric-but-not-policy

## 17. She Will Fight for Equal Pay

[1] http://www.nydailynews.com/news/world/hillary-clinton-women-world-summit-womens-rights-unfinished-business-21st-century-article-1.1308691
[2] http://www.reviewjournal.com/business/money/4-ways-equal-pay-equal-work-benefits-both-women-and-men
[3] http://makeitworkcampaign.org/issues/equal-pay/
[4] https://www.hillaryclinton.com/the-briefing/fact-sheet-equal-pay/
[5] http://www.huffingtonpost.com/entry/donald-trump-equal-pay-womp-womp_us_561d2079e4b050c6c4a2d888
[6] http://www.huffingtonpost.com/2015/05/27/hillary-clinton-equal-pay_n_7454096.html
[7] https://www.hillaryclinton.com/the-briefing/fact-sheet-equal-pay/
[8] http://www.iwpr.org/publications/pubs/how-equal-pay-for-working-women-would-reduce-poverty-and-grow-the-american-economy/

## 18. She Will Ensure That All Americans Have Access to Healthcare

[1] http://www.cnn.com/2015/09/20/politics/hillary-clinton-obamacare-fixes/
[2] http://kff.org/uninsured/issue-brief/a-closer-look-at-the-remaining-uninsured-population-eligible-for-medicaid-and-chip/
[3] https://www.hillaryclinton.com/issues/health-care/
[4] http://www.ontheissues.org/Hillary_Clinton.htm#Health_Care
[5] https://www.hillaryclinton.com/issues/health-care/
[6] http://www.pbs.org/program/us-health-care-good-news/
[7] http://www.nytimes.com/2015/10/07/us/politics/hillary-clintons-proposed-changes-to-health-law-zero-in-on-affordability.html
[8] http://www.nytimes.com/2015/10/07/us/politics/hillary-clintons-proposed-changes-to-health-law-zero-in-on-affordability.html
[9] https://www.hillaryclinton.com/p/briefing/factsheets/2015/09/21/hillary-clinton-plan-for-lowering-prescription-drug-costs/
[10] http://www.rgj.com/story/opinion/voices/2015/07/14/op-ed-hillary-will-fight-veterans/30145365/
[11] https://www.washingtonpost.com/opinions/dana-milbank-with-latest-obamacare-repeal-vote-gop-sets-record-for-futility/2015/02/03/26a4266c-abf2-11e4-9c91-e9d2f9fde644_story.html
[12] http://www.cnn.com/2013/09/18/politics/obamacare-government-shutdown/
[13] https://www.washingtonpost.com/politics/health-law-repeal-and-replace-joins-republican-presidential-contest/2015/08/18/b620ee94-45ce-11e5-846d-02792f854297_story.html

## 19. She Will Pick Fair and Just Supreme Court Nominees

[1] http://www.thenation.com/article/hillary-clinton-just-delivered-the-strongest-speech-of-her-campaign-and-the-media-barely-noticed/
[2] http://www.thenation.com/article/hillary-clinton-just-delivered-the-strongest-speech-of-her-campaign-and-the-media-barely-noticed/

[3] http://www.publicpolicypolling.com/main/2016/05/americans-dont-trust-trump-on-supreme-court-vacancy-65-want-hearings.html

## 20. She Will Fight for Fair Taxes for American Families

[1] http://time.com/3920332/transcript-full-text-hillary-clinton-campaign-launch/transcript.html?action=click&contentCollection=Politics&module=RelatedCoverage&region=Marginalia&pgtype=article
[2] http://money.cnn.com/2013/03/04/news/economy/buffett-secretary-taxes/
[3]http://www.senate.gov/legislative/LIS/roll_call_lists/roll_call_vote_cfm.cfm?congress=107&session=1&vote=00170
[4] http://money.cnn.com/2012/01/03/news/economy/income_inequality/
[5] http://web.archive.org/web/20081205045818/http:/clinton.senate.gov/news/statements/details.cfm?id=235141&&
[6] http://www.nytimes.com/2007/07/14/business/14tax.html?pagewanted=print&_r=0
[7] https://www.hillaryclinton.com/p/briefing/factsheets/2015/10/08/wall-street-work-for-main-street/
[8] https://www.hillaryclinton.com/p/briefing/factsheets/2015/08/10/college-compact-costs/
[9] https://www.linkedin.com/pulse/four-ways-jump-start-small-business-hillary-clinton
[10] http://www.nytimes.com/2015/10/17/business/putting-numbers-to-a-tax-increase-for-the-rich.html
[11] http://www.washingtonpost.com/news/wonkblog/wp/2015/04/27/for-every-problem-republicans-have-a-solution-tax-cuts/

## 21. She Will Create a Criminal Justice System That Works

[1] http://www.vox.com/2015/4/29/8514831/hillary-clinton-criminal-justice-transcript
[2] http://www.cbsnews.com/news/the-cost-of-a-nation-of-incarceration/
[3] http://www.cbsnews.com/news/the-cost-of-a-nation-of-incarceration/
[4] http://www.cbsnews.com/news/the-cost-of-a-nation-of-incarceration/
[5] Spohn, Cassia, "Thirty Years of Sentencing Reform: The Quest for a Racially Neutral Sentencing Process," W. Reed and L. Winterfield, eds., *Criminal Justice 2000* (Washington, D.C.: National Institute of Justice, 2001), vol. 3, pp. 427-501.
[6] https://www.congress.gov/bill/107th-congress/senate-bill/989/cosponsors; https://www.congress.gov/bill/108th-congress/senate-bill/2132/cosponsors
[7] http://web.archive.org/web/20080528220552/http:/www.hillaryclinton.com/news/speech/view/?id=2645
[8] http://www.vox.com/2015/4/29/8514831/hillary-clinton-criminal-justice-transcript
[9] http://www.vox.com/2015/4/29/8514831/hillary-clinton-criminal-justice-transcript
[10] https://www.hillaryclinton.com/issues/criminal-justice-reform/
[11] http://static.nicic.gov/Library/017624.pdf
[12] http://www.usatoday.com/story/news/politics/elections/2015/04/29/hillary-clinton-body-cameras-baltimore/26569575/

[13] http://www.nbcnews.com/news/nbcblk/hillary-clinton-targets-hbcus-college-affordability-plan-n410591

[14] http://www.nwlc.org/resource/closing-wage-gap-crucial-women-color-and-their-families

## III. Human Dignity

## 22. She Believes in a Roadmap to Citizenship

[1] http://www.cbsnews.com/news/hillary-clinton-heckled-by-immigration-protesters/

[2] Gallup Poll, June 15-July 10, 2015, N=2,296 adults nationwide. Margin of error ± 4.

[3] http://thomas.loc.gov/cgi-bin/query/z?r110:S24OC7-0015:

[4] https://www.congress.gov/crec/2007/06/06/CREC-2007-06-06-pt1-PgS7099-3.pdf

[5] http://www.hhs.gov/healthcare/facts/blog/2014/02/celebrating-five-years-of-chipra.html

[6] https://www.congress.gov/crec/2003/07/31/CREC-2003-07-31-pt2-PgS10621.pdf

[7] http://www.nytimes.com/politics/first-draft/2015/10/06/hillary-clinton-plans-a-more-humane-approach-on-immigration/?_r=0

[8] http://www.dhs.gov/xlibrary/assets/statistics/publications/ois_ill_pe_2011.pdf

[9] http://www.cnn.com/2015/12/07/politics/donald-trump-muslim-ban-immigration/

[10] http://americanactionforum.org/research/the-budgetary-and-economic-costs-of-addressing-unauthorized-immigration-alt

[11] Meissner, Doris Donald M. Kerwin, Muzaffar Chishti, and Claire Bergeron, *Immigration Enforcement in the United States: The Rise of a Formidable Machinery* (Washington, DC: Migration Policy Institute, 2013).

[12] http://www.immigrationpolicy.org/sites/default/files/docs/Hinojosa%20-%20Raising%20the%20Floor%20for%20American%20Workers%20010710.pdf

[13] https://www.americanprogress.org/issues/immigration/report/2014/10/23/59040/the-facts-on-immigration-today-3/

## 23. She Will Fight to Eliminate Violence Against Women

[1] http://www.theguardian.com/commentisfree/2011/dec/10/violence-women-hillary-clinton

[2] http://www.ncadv.org/learn/statistics; http://www.cnn.com/2013/12/06/us/domestic-intimate-partner-violence-fast-facts/

[3] http://www.unwomen.org/en/what-we-do/ending-violence-against-women/facts-and-figures

[4] http://www.ncadv.org/learn/statistics

[5] http://www.bustle.com/articles/108930-7-memorable-quotes-from-hillary-clintons-1995-womens-rights-speech-that-are-still-meaningful-today

[6] http://www.pbs.org/wgbh/americanexperience/features/biography/clinton-hillary/

[7] http://www.theatlantic.com/politics/archive/2015/05/the-tragic-politics-of-crime/392114/

[8] http://www.pbs.org/wgbh/americanexperience/features/biography/clinton-hillary/

[9] Clinton, Hillary Rodham, *Hard Choices* (New York: Simon & Schuster, 2014) 572

[10] http://www.nsvrc.org/saam/campus-resource-list

[11] https://www.hillaryclinton.com/issues/campus-sexual-assault/

[12] http://time.com/2895141/hillary-clinton-military-sexual-assault/

[13] http://servicewomen.org/wp-content/uploads/2011/01/SWAN-MST-fact-sheet1.pdf

## 24. She Believes That Black Lives Matter

[1] http://www.bustle.com/articles/99029-these-7-hillary-clinton-quotes-on-race-relations-prove-that-she-gets-it-or-is-at

[2] http://www.theroot.com/articles/culture/2014/10/young_black_men_21_times_more_likely_to_be_shot_dead_by_police_than_whites.html

[3] http://www.theguardian.com/us-news/2015/jun/01/black-americans-killed-by-police-analysis

[4] Spohn, Cassia, "Thirty Years of Sentencing Reform: The Quest for a Racially Neutral Sentencing Process," W. Reed and L. Winterfield, eds., *Criminal Justice 2000* (Washington, D.C.: National Institute of Justice, 2001), vol. 3, pp. 427-501.

[5] https://www.congress.gov/bill/107th-congress/senate-bill/989/cosponsors; https://www.congress.gov/bill/108th-congress/senate-bill/2132/cosponsors

[6] http://web.archive.org/web/20080528220552/http:/www.hillaryclinton.com/news/speech/view/?id=2645

[7] http://web.archive.org/web/20080529023640/http:/www.hillaryclinton.com/news/release/view/?id=7033

[8] http://www.vox.com/2015/4/29/8514831/hillary-clinton-criminal-justice-transcript

[9] http://www.nbcnews.com/news/nbcblk/hillary-clinton-targets-hbcus-college-affordability-plan-n410591

[10] http://www.nwlc.org/resource/closing-wage-gap-crucial-women-color-and-their-families

## 25. She Cares About Our Veterans

[1] http://freebeacon.com/issues/flashback-hillary-clinton-says-presidents-highest-obligation-is-to-care-for-veterans/

[2] http://www.usnews.com/news/blogs/data-mine/2014/11/10/veterans-day-data-boot-camp

[3] http://nchv.org/index.php/news/media/background_and_statistics/

[4] http://www.bls.gov/news.release/pdf/vet.pdf

[5] http://www.tbbf.org/22-veterans-commit-suicide-daily/08-2014#pk_campaign=GA2481?matchtype=b&keyword=22%20veterans%20a%20day%20commit%20suicide&adposition=1t1

[6] http://www.rgj.com/story/opinion/voices/2015/07/14/op-ed-hillary—fight-veterans/30145365/

[7] http://thomas.loc.gov/cgi-bin/bdquery/D?d110:3:./temp/~bd6eDo:@@@P

[8] http://www.politico.com/story/2015/06/hillary-clinton-work-well-lindsey-graham-john-mccain-119048

[9] http://thehill.com/policy/defense/247998-clinton-reaching-out-to-military-veterans
[10] https://www.fas.org/sgp/crs/misc/R42755.pdf
[11] http://time.com/3927668/hillary-clinton-veterans-college/
[12] http://www.rgj.com/story/opinion/voices/2015/07/14/op-ed-hillary—fight-veterans/30145365/
[13] https://www.hillaryclinton.com/issues/veterans/
[14] http://www.politicususa.com/2015/11/11/republicans-congress-dishonoring-americas-veterans.html

## 26. She Will Combat Gun Violence

[1] http://www.cbsnews.com/news/hillary-clinton-mass-shootings-beyond-my-comprehension/
[2] http://www.bradycampaign.org/key-gun-violence-statistics
[3] https://www.washingtonpost.com/news/the-fix/wp/2015/08/27/hillary-clinton-is-the-new-standard-bearer-for-gun-control-so-lets-look-at-her-record/
[4] Sisk, Richard, "Secretary of State Hillary Clinton's Call for Assault Weapon Ban in U.S. Gets Blasted by Gun Lobby," *New York Daily News*, March 26, 2009.
[5] http://www.nytimes.com/1999/05/11/us/clinton-holds-youth-violence-summit.html
[6] https://www.congress.gov/bill/107th-congress/senate-bill/890/cosponsors; https://www.congress.gov/bill/108th-congress/senate-bill/1807/cosponsors
[7] https://www.hillaryclinton.com/p/briefing/factsheets/2015/10/04/clinton-believes-its-time-to-tackle-gun-violence/
[8] Office of the Inspector General, Evaluation and Inspections Division, U.S. Department of Justice, *Review of ATF's Federal Firearms Licensee Inspection Program*,April 2013.
[9] http://www.msnbc.com/msnbc/majority-americans-support-background-checks-poll-says
[10] http://www.businessinsider.com/hillary-clinton-gun-control-plan-2015-10
[11] http://www.theguardian.com/us-news/2015/oct/05/hillary-clinton-unveils-plan-for-tougher-checks-in-bid-to-reduce-gun-violence

## 27. She Will Fight for LGBT Rights in the US and Worldwide

[1] https://www.hillaryclinton.com/p/briefing/factsheets/2015/08/06/clinton-gop-lgbt-rights/
[2] http://time.com/3938898/hillary-clinton-gay-marriage/
[3] https://www.congress.gov/bill/107th-congress/senate-bill/1284/cosponsors
[4] https://www.congress.gov/bill/110th-congress/senate-bill/1105/cosponsors
[5] http://www.ohchr.org/EN/NewsEvents/Pages/DisplayNews.aspx?NewsID=11167&LangID=E
[6] Clinton, Hillary Rodham, *Hard Choices* (New York: Simon & Schuster, 2014), 578.http://www.nytimes.com/2009/05/24/us/24benefit.html
[7] http://foreignpolicy.com/2010/06/10/state-department-transgender-passports-now-available/
[8] http://www.huffingtonpost.com/entry/hillary-clinton-equality-act_55b12877e4b08f57d5d3ed54
[9] http://www.dailydot.com/politics/equality-act-2015-lgbt-explained/

[10] http://www.huffingtonpost.com/entry/hillary-clinton-equality-act_55b12877e4b08f57d5d3ed54
[11] http://www.washingtonexaminer.com/hillary-clinton-confronts-religious-freedom-laws-including-her-husbands/article/2562448
[12] https://www.hillaryclinton.com/p/briefing/factsheets/2015/08/06/clinton-gop-lgbt-rights/
[13] http://www.cnn.com/2015/06/30/politics/cnn-poll-iran-scotus/index.html
[14] http://www.hrc.org/blog/entry/poll-59-of-voters-less-likely-to-support-candidates-who-oppose-non-discrimi
[15] https://www.hillaryclinton.com/p/briefing/factsheets/2015/08/06/clinton-gop-lgbt-rights/
[16] http://www.hrc.org/2016RepublicanFacts/ted-cruz
[17] http://www.hrc.org/2016RepublicanFacts/donald-trump

## 28. She Will Take Care of Our Seniors

[1] http://www.presidency.ucsb.edu/ws/?pid=92373
[2] http://thomas.loc.gov/cgi-bin/bdquery/D?d110:26:./temp/~bdBNrF::
[3] New York 2006 Senate Debate, at University of Rochester Oct 22, 2006
[4] http://www.ontheissues.org/SenateVote/Party_2008-S177.htm
[5] http://thomas.loc.gov/cgi-bin/bdquery/z?d110:SN00003:
[6] http://www.usatoday.com/story/money/personalfinance/2016/03/07/how-presidential-candidates-would-change-social-security/81178142/
[7] http://www.latimes.com/business/hiltzik/la-fi-mh-clinton-social-security-20151014-column.html
[8] http://fightfor15homecare.org/caregap-post/
[9] http://static.politico.com/54/24/77b932744dbe80c0b496dec2eedb/hillary-clinton-caregiver-tax-plan.pdf
[10] http://www.huffingtonpost.com/2015/05/11/hillary-clinton-paid-family-leave-mothers-day_n_7257370.html

## 29. She Will Fix Our Broken Mental Health System

[1] https://www.hillaryclinton.com/speeches/official-campaign-launch-speech-new-york-citys-roosevelt-island/
[2] http://www2.nami.org/factsheets/mentalillness_factsheet.pdf
[3] http://www.ncbi.nlm.nih.gov/pmc/articles/PMC4318286/
[4] https://www.congress.gov/congressional-record/2005/05/25/senate-section/article/S5923-1
[5] https://www.congress.gov/bill/109th-congress/senate-bill/3517
[6] http://www2.nami.org/factsheets/mentalillness_factsheet.pdf
[7] http://www2.nami.org/factsheets/mentalillness_factsheet.pdf

## 30. She Will Fight for Women Around the World

[1] http://www.hillaryhq.com/2015/05/women-in-world-summit-2015-keynote.html
[2] http://www.un.org/esa/gopher-data/conf/fwcw/conf/gov/950905175653.txt
[3] http://www.politico.com/blogs/politico44/2013/03/obama-picks-new-ambassador-

at-large-for-womens-issues-159640
[4] https://www.georgetown.edu/news/hillary-clinton-security-inclusive-leadership.html
[5] http://www.huffingtonpost.com/andrea-dew-steele/why-hillary-clinton-has-t_b_8073982.html
[6] https://www.hillaryclinton.com/issues/womens-rights-and-opportunity/
[7] https://www.opendemocracy.net/openglobalrights/elsy-melkonian/women%E2%80%99s-rights-in-tunisia-promising-future-or-religiopolitical-game
[8] http://www.cnn.com/2015/08/21/world/saudi-arabia-women-voting/
[9] http://www.state.gov/secretary/20092013clinton/rm/2011/05/164329.htm
[10] http://www.self.com/work/politics/2015/04/timeline-how-hillary-clinton-has-paved-the-way-for-womens-rights/
[11] http://time.com/16868/clinton-kicks-off-international-womens-day-at-united-nations/
[12] http://www.nbcnews.com/politics/2016-election/clinton-roll-out-plan-combat-sexual-assault-colleges-n427016

## 31. She Will Tackle Substance Abuse

[1] Clinton, Hillary, "Another View—Hillary Clinton: How We Can Win the Fight against Substance Abuse," *New Hampshire Union Leader*, September 1, 2015.
[2] United States, National Institute of Health, National Institute on Drug Abuse, *DrugFacts: Nationwide Trends*, June 2015.
[3] http://correctrecord.org/hillary-clinton-a-record-of-service-to-veterans/
[4] http://www.unionleader.com/apps/pbcs.dll/article?AID=/20150901/OPINION02/150909909
[5] http://www.dscc.org/pressrelease/kelly-ayotte-refuses-fight-against-republicans-deep-cuts-substance-abuse-treatment-and

## 32. She Will Protect the Rights of Americans with Disabilities

[1] https://www.hillaryclinton.com/p/briefing/statements/2015/07/26/ada-anniversary-statement/
[2] http://www.childrensdefense.org/newsroom/cdf-in-the-news/press-releases/2013/honoring-hillary-clinton.html
[3] https://www.govtrack.us/congress/bills/110/s3406/summary
[4] http://thomas.loc.gov/cgi-bin/bdquery/D?d110:36:./temp/~bdK66m::

## 33. She Will Fight for Human Rights Around the World

[1] http://edition.cnn.com/2015/01/21/politics/hillary-clinton-canada-future-vision/
[2] Kelley, Colleen, *The Rhetoric of First Lady Hillary Rodham Clinton: Crisis Management Discourse*, (Westport, CT: Praeger, 2001).
[3] Sally Bedell Smith, "For Love of Politics," October 23, 2007, 215-216 [4]http://exhibits.lib.usf.edu/exhibits/show/darfur-genocide/modeofdestruction/rape
[5]http://www.aaainc.org/fileadmin/aaainc/pdf_2008/Armenia_Statement_of_Senator_Hillary_Clinton.pdf

[6] http://www.washingtonpost.com/wp-dyn/content/article/2007/09/27/AR2007092701730.html
[7] http://www.state.gov/secretary/20092013clinton/rm/2009a/02/119786.htm
[8] http://www.state.gov/r/pa/prs/ps/2011/03/159343.htm
[9] http://www.state.gov/secretary/20092013clinton/rm/2012/12/201618.htm
[10] http://thehill.com/blogs/ballot-box/presidential-races/308269-jeb-bush-to-present-award-to-hillary-clinton
[11] http://www.aljazeera.com/news/2016/03/donald-trump-backpedals-torture-pledge-160305034524423.html
[12] http://www.politico.com/blogs/new-hampshire-primary-2016-live-updates/2016/02/ted-cruz-waterboarding-2016-debate-218879

## IV. Freedom

### 34. She Will Break ISIS

[1] http://time.com/4120295/hillary-clinton-foreign-policy-isis/
[2] http://www.dailymail.co.uk/news/article-2719991/Horrific-new-photographs-ISIS-atrocities-prompted-Obama-act.html
[3] http://www.businessinsider.com/isis-message-tashfeen-malik-posted-on-facebook-during-attack-2015-12
[4] http://nypost.com/2012/08/21/hill-swayed-o-to-kill-osama/
[5] Clinton, Hillary Rodham, *Hard Choices* (New York: Simon & Schuster, 2014), 391.
[6] https://www.thegctf.org/web/guest/members-and-partners
[7] http://www.state.gov/secretary/20092013clinton/rm/2011/09/172034.htm
[8] http://time.com/4120295/hillary-clinton-foreign-policy-isis/
[9] https://www.rt.com/usa/322785-hillary-clinton-isis-strategy/
[10] http://time.com/4120295/hillary-clinton-foreign-policy-isis/
[11] https://www.rt.com/usa/322785-hillary-clinton-isis-strategy/
[12] http://www.politico.com/story/2015/09/hillary-clinton-syria-refugees-213444
[13] http://thehill.com/policy/national-security/263328-clinton-challenges-gop-bluster-and-bigotry-before-debate

### 35. She Believes in Using Smart Power Abroad

[1] http://www.washingtontimes.com/news/2014/dec/3/hillary-clinton-smart-show-respect-even-enemies/
[2] http://csis.org/files/media/csis/pubs/071106_csissmartpowerreport.pdf
[3] http://www.state.gov/secretary/20092013clinton/rm/2009a/01/115196.htm
[4] http://www.politifact.com/truth-o-meter/statements/2015/nov/23/hillary-clinton/hillary-clinton-says-she-helped-usher-iran-negotia/
[5] http://www.worldpublicopinion.org/pipa/2013%20Country%20Rating%20Poll.pdf
[6] http://thediplomat.com/2015/10/how-the-global-maritime-fulcrum-can-elevate-the-us-indonesia-partnership/
[7] http://www.washingtontimes.com/news/2014/dec/3/hillary-clinton-smart-show-respect-even-enemies/
[8] http://www.state.gov/secretary/20092013clinton/rm/2011/12/179173.htm

## 36. She Will Balance Security and Privacy

[1] http://www.thenation.com/article/6-degrees-separation-between-bernie-sanders-and-hillary-clinton/

[2] http://engine.is/wp-content/uploads/2016-Candidate-Report-Card.pdf

[3] http://engine.is/wp-content/uploads/2016-Candidate-Report-Card.pdf

[4] http://thomas.loc.gov/cgi-bin/query/z?c107:H.R.3162.enr:

[5] http://www.senate.gov/legislative/LIS/roll_call_lists/roll_call_vote_cfm.cfm?congress=109&session=2&vote=00029

[6] http://web.archive.org/web/20060627112300/http://www.senate.gov/~clinton/news/statements/details.cfm?id=249895

[7] http://www.state.gov/secretary/20092013clinton/rm/2010/01/135519.htm

[8] http://www.npr.org/sections/thetwo-way/2015/06/02/411534447/senateis-poised-to-vote-on-house-approved-usa-freedom-act?utm_source=twitter.com&utm_campaign=npr&utm_medium=social&utm_term=nprnews

[9] http://www.msnbc.com/msnbc/hillary-clinton-endorses-nsa-reform-bill

[10] http://www.ibtimes.com/hillary-clinton-calls-internet-freedom-core-value-dreamforce-conference-1705158

[11] http://blogs.wsj.com/washwire/2015/07/28/hillary-clinton-wants-islamic-state-off-twitter/

[12] http://time.com/4120295/hillary-clinton-foreign-policy-isis/

## 37. She Stands With Israel

[1] http://www.state.gov/secretary/20092013clinton/rm/2012/11/201343.htm

[2] http://shabak.gov.il/SiteCollectionImages/english/TerrorInfo/reports/2010summary2-en.pdf

[3] http://thomas.loc.gov/cgi-bin/bdquery/z?d109:SN02370:

[4] http://www.nytimes.com/2010/02/17/world/middleeast/17diplo.html

[5] http://www.c-span.org/video/?204894-1/pennsylvania-democratic-presidential-candidates-debate

[6] https://www.hillaryclinton.com/p/briefing/factsheets/2015/09/08/israel-friendship-leadership-strength/

[7] http://www.i24news.tv/en/news/international/americas/67519-150413-hillary-clinton-s-policy-towards-israel

[8] http://www.cnn.com/2015/09/09/politics/hillary-clinton-iran-nuclear-deal/

## 38. She Will Restore American Leadership in Asia

[1.] Clinton, Hillary, "America's Pacific Century," *Foreign Policy*, November 2011.

[2] https://www.washingtonpost.com/news/worldviews/wp/2015/10/12/hillary-clintons-long-and-complicated-relationship-with-china/

[3] http://www.nytimes.com/1995/09/06/world/hillary-clinton-in-china-details-abuse-of-women.html

[4] http://www.state.gov/secretary/20092013clinton/rm/2009a/12/133544.htm

[5] http://www.bbc.com/news/world-asia-china-34377406

[6] http://www.brookings.edu/research/opinions/2013/12/13-asia-rebalance-ohanlon

[7] http://www.forbes.com/2010/07/28/china-beijing-asia-hillary-clinton-opinions-

columnists-gordon-g-chang.html

[8] http://www.washingtontimes.com/news/2015/jul/23/hillary-clinton-blasts-china-us-trade-woes/

[9] http://thediplomat.com/2014/02/new-report-could-offer-clues-to-hillary-clintons-china-policy/

[10] https://cdn.americanprogress.org/wp-content/uploads/2014/02/ChinaReport-Full.pdf

## 39. She Will Protect Women's Reproductive Health

[1] http://abcnews.go.com/Politics/hillary-clinton-jeb-bush-duke-womens-health-issues/story?id=32893768

[2] http://www.nytimes.com/1993/01/20/us/the-inauguration-the-first-couple-a-union-of-mind-and-ambition.html?pagewanted=2

[3] Bernstein, Carl, *A Woman in Charge: The Life of Hillary Rodham Clinton* (New York: Alfred A. Knopf, 2007), 256-257.

[4] Clinton, Hillary Rodham, *It Takes a Village: And Other Lessons Children Teach Us* (New York: Simon & Schuster, 2006),306.

[5] https://votesmart.org/public-statement/85138/reid-and-clinton-detail-prevention-first-amendment#.Vi50ddKrTIU

[6] https://web.archive.org/web/20071021054633/http://naral.org/elections/statements/clinton.html

[7] http://www.politico.com/story/2015/08/hillary-clinton-video-ad-support-planned-parenthood-2016-120949#ixzz3qNM34HFQ

[8] https://www.hillaryclinton.com/issues/womens-rights-and-opportunity/

[9] http://www.nytimes.com/2015/05/28/opinion/supreme-court-litmus-testing-in-the-2016-election.html

[10] http://www.salon.com/2016/03/09/donald_trump_may_be_an_actual_fascist_ted_cruz_is_still_more_dangerous_partner/

[11] http://www.pfaw.org/media-center/publications/gop-takes-its-war-women-states

# V. Perseverance

## 40. She Is the Most Experienced

[1] http://www.chicagotribune.com/news/local/politics/ct-bill-clinton-illinois-primary-rally-met-0309-20160308-story.html

[2] http://www.wbur.org/2015/03/19/hillary-clinton-presidential-qualifications

[3] http://www.politifact.com/truth-o-meter/statements/2015/aug/07/marco-rubio/rubio-says-hillary-clinton-office-longer-any-repub/

[4] https://www.hillaryclinton.com/feed/seven-hillary-clintons-biggest-accomplishments/

[5] https://www.hillaryclinton.com/about/bio/

[6] http://www.politico.com/story/2014/09/henry-kissinger-praise-hillary-clinton-110755

[7] https://www.washingtonpost.com/blogs/fact-checker/post/hillary-clintons-overseas-diplomacy-versus-other-secretaries-of-state/2013/01/08/742f46b2-59f3-11e2-9fa9-5fbdc9530eb9_blog.html

## 41. She Can Win

[1] http://time.com/3920332/transcript-full-text-hillary-clinton-campaign-launch/
[2] http://www.nytimes.com/2015/05/06/us/politics/hillary-clinton-gains-favor-times-cbs-pollnd-says.html
[3] https://www.washingtonpost.com/blogs/plum-line/wp/2015/07/10/the-demographics-of-2016-look-brutal-for-republicans/
[4] http://presidentialgenderwatch.org/the-rising-american-electorate-game-changers-in-2016-elections/
[5] http://www.usatoday.com/story/news/politics/elections/2016/03/14/poll-millennials-clinton-sanders-trump-president/81612520/
[6] http://fivethirtyeight.com/features/donald-trump-is-really-unpopular-with-general-election-voters/
[7] https://www.washingtonpost.com/politics/poll-clinton-leads-trump-aided-by-obama-coalition/2016/03/08/40dd6698-e575-11e5-b0fd-073d5930a7b7_story.html
[8] http://www.usatoday.com/story/news/politics/elections/2016/03/14/poll-millennials-clinton-sanders-trump-president/81612520/

## 42. She's a Mother and a Grandmother

[1] http://www.bustle.com/articles/96815-the-single-hillary-clinton-quote-from-her-economic-policy-speech-thats-the-real-cornerstone-of-her
[2] http://www.thewrap.com/chelsea-clinton-endorses-mom-teases-her-own-political-ambitions-video/
[3] http://www.makers.com/hillary-rodham-clinton
[4] http://www.amazon.com/exec/obidos/ASIN/0688157491/issues2000org/
[5] http://www.techrepublic.com/article/10-things-you-need-to-know-about-maternity-leave-in-the-us/
[6] https://www.hillaryclinton.com/issues/womens-rights-and-opportunity/
[7] https://www.hillaryclinton.com/issues/early-childhood-education/
[8] Clinton, Hillary Rodham, *Hard Choices* (New York: Simon & Schuster, 2014).
[9] http://www.cnn.com/2015/09/12/politics/hillary-clinton-charlotte-tv-ad/

## 43. She Knows the World

[1] http://www.cntraveler.com/stories/2012-08-13/hillary-clinton
[2] http://www.csmonitor.com/USA/Foreign-Policy/2012/0905/Hillary-Clinton-vs.-Condi-Rice-Who-gets-the-most-traveled-crown
[3] http://www.theatlantic.com/politics/archive/2013/01/hillary-clinton-traveled-956-733-miles-during-her-time-as-secretary-of-state/272656/
[4] http://abcnews.go.com/Politics/departing-secretary-state-hillary-clinton-leaves-legacy-firsts/story?id=18039755&singlePage=true
[5] http://www.dailykos.com/story/2015/9/17/1422129/-Hillary-s-Accomplishments-2012-Ceasefire
[6] http://www.npr.org/sections/itsallpolitics/2014/06/10/320482083/hillary-clinton-i-helped-restore-u-s-leadership-in-the-world
[7] http://www.usatoday.com/story/news/world/2016/03/08/donald-trump-world-leaders-republican-gop/81312520/

## 44. She's Badass

[1] http://nymag.com/daily/intelligencer/2013/06/hillary-clinton-pantsuit-jokes-video-history-list.html

[2] http://time.com/3940783/hillary-clinton-terry-mcauliffe-robby-mook/

[3] http://www.people.com/article/hillary-clinton-dances-nae-nae-ellen

[4] https://www.instagram.com/p/3wNnxBEPpX/

[5] http://www.cntraveler.com/stories/2012-08-30/hillary-clinton-interview-visionaries

[6] http://www.washingtonpost.com/blogs/she-the-people/post/hillary-clinton-is-finally-hip-thanks-to-meme/2012/04/12/gIQALzOODT_blog.html

[7] http://www.breitbart.com/big-government/2015/04/13/hillary-spotted-at-chipotle-wears-sunglasses-indoors/

[8] http://www.nydailynews.com/news/politics/hillary-clinton-win-williamsburg-hipsters-article-1.2521510

[9] http://greatideas.people.com/2015/09/29/hillary-clinton-pumpkin-spice-latte/

[10] http://www.forbes.com/2007/08/30/women-power-speech-biz-07women-cz_em_0830speak.html

[11] http://www.politico.com/story/2015/07/hillary-clinton-campaign-2016-gender-card-mitch-mcconnell-120400#ixzz3p8cfMRVi

[12] http://abcnews.go.com/GMA/Politics/story?id=8297962

[13] https://books.google.com/books?id=V_YcAwAAQBAJ&pg=PA106&lpg=PA106&dq=I%E2%80%99m+sick+and+tired+of+people+who+say+that+if+you+debate+and+disagree+with+this+administration&source=bl&ots=jPJD3SfUl3&sig=BzIDOLCsd9EN2sZ7Ks2PvhxpOCk&hl=en&sa=X&ved=0CCIQ6AEwAjgKahUKEwiEify-99HIAhXJf5AKHQy4DHg#v=onepage&q=I%E2%80%99m%20sick%20and%20tired%20of%20people%20who%20say%20that%20if%20you%20debate%20and%20disagree%20with%20this%20administration&f=false

[14] https://newrepublic.com/article/122035/meet-new-old-hillary-clinton

[15] http://theweek.com/speedreads/611770/hillary-clinton-not-natural-politician

## 45. She's a Midwesterner

[1] http://www.cbsnews.com/news/clinton-says-obama-is-out-of-touch-with-middle-class-americans-calls-comments-elitist/

[2] http://www.wsj.com/articles/for-peripatetic-hillary-clinton-the-midwest-becomes-home-1408556187

[3] Bernstein, Carl, *A Woman in Charge: The Life of Hillary Rodham Clinton* (New York: Alfred A. Knopf, 2007), 34

[4] http://www.nytimes.com/2015/07/20/us/politics/hillary-clinton-draws-scrappy-determination-from-a-tough-combative-father.html

[5] http://www.vox.com/2015/6/13/8776067/hillary-clinton-transcript-campaign-launch

[6] http://www.nytimes.com/2015/07/20/us/politics/hillary-clinton-draws-scrappy-determination-from-a-tough-combative-father.html

[7] http://thinkprogress.org/economy/2015/09/02/3697832/epi-wages-productivity/

[8] http://www.wsj.com/articles/hillary-clinton-gives-details-of-worker-profit-sharing-proposal-1437081856

[9] https://www.hillaryclinton.com/issues/small-business/
[10] http://www.nytimes.com/2015/06/13/us/politics/story-of-hillary-clintons-mother-forms-emotional-core-of-campaign.html
[11] http://time.com/3920332/transcript-full-text-hillary-clinton-campaign-launch/

## 46. She Turned Bill Down (At First)

[1] http://us11.campaign-archive2.com/?u=a5b04a26aae05a24bc4efb63e&id=66c-4dad14b
[2] http://abcnews.go.com/2020/story?id=123702&page=1
[3] http://www.salon.com/2012/09/02/when_bill_met_hillary/ee
[4] https://www.theknot.com/content/hillary-and-bill-clinton-wedding-story
[5] http://www.pewsocialtrends.org/files/2012/04/Women-in-the-Workplace.pdf
[6] http://www.politico.com/story/2015/08/hillary-clinton-video-ad-support-planned-parenHthood-2016-120949
[7] http://www.cbsnews.com/news/bill-and-hillary-clinton-celebrate-40-years-of-marriage/
[8] http://www.nytimes.com/2015/06/13/us/politics/story-of-hillary-clintons-mother-forms-emotional-core-of-campaign.html

## 47. She Admits When She's Wrong

[1] http://time.com/3920332/transcript-full-text-hillary-clinton-campaign-launch/
[2] http://www.senate.gov/legislative/LIS/roll_call_lists/roll_call_vote_cfm.cfm?congress=107&session=2&vote=00237
[3] http://nation.time.com/2012/09/06/iraq-how-the-cia-says-it-blew-it-on-saddams-wmd/
[4] http://www.huffingtonpost.com/daniel-raphael/the-failure-of-the-iraq-w_b_5530820.html
[5] http://www.politico.com/story/2015/05/hillary-clinton-iraq-war-vote-mistake-iowa-118109#ixzz3qT4xZwlq
[6] http://www.ontheissues.org/Archive/2007_HRC_LOGO_Hillary_Clinton.htm
[7] http://www.politifact.com/truth-o-meter/statements/2015/jun/17/hillary-clinton/hillary-clinton-change-position-same-sex-marriage/
[8] http://www.cnn.com/2015/09/09/politics/hillary-clinton-email-apology/
[9] http://www.washingtontimes.com/news/2016/feb/13/15-percent-latest-hillary-clinton-emails-marked-cl/
[10] https://www.washingtonpost.com/news/post-politics/wp/2015/09/08/hillary-clinton-apologizes-for-e-mail-system-i-take-responsibility/
[11] http://www.cnn.com/2016/02/04/politics/hillary-clinton-email-classified-colin-powell-condoleezza-rice/
[12] http://www.huffingtonpost.com/entry/donald-trump-explains-doesnt-apologize_55f434cce4b077ca094f4bf5

## 48. She Is the Most Admired Woman in America

[1] https://www.youtube.com/watch?v=uD9pOyUwe3I&feature=youtu.be
[2] http://thehill.com/blogs/ballot-box/presidential-races/264292-poll-clinton-is-

americas-most-admired-woman

[3] http://www.cnsnews.com/news/article/penny-starr/madeleine-albright-hillary-clintons-greatest-accomplishment-secretary-state

[4] http://www.foxnews.com/on-air/on-the-record/2013/01/24/mccain-even-clintons-testimony-there-are-still-so-many-unanswered-questions-benghazi

[5] http://www.politico.com/story/2014/09/henry-kissinger-praise-hillary-clinton-110755

[6] https://www.youtube.com/watch?v=-GzGAW7k2V8

[7] https://www.youtube.com/watch?v=-GzGAW7k2V8&feature=youtu.be

## 49. She Can Work with Republicans

[1] http://correctrecord.org/hillary-clintons-bipartisanship/

[2] http://www.nbcnews.com/politics/2016-election/clinton-sanders-spar-start-democratic-debate-n444031

[3] http://www.npr.org/sections/itsallpolitics/2015/04/11/395302391/5-things-you-should-know-about-hillary-clinton

[4] https://www.washingtonpost.com/news/the-fix/wp/2015/05/05/when-hillary-clinton-was-a-republican-and-rick-perry-was-a-democrat/

[5] http://www.epw.senate.gov/public/index.cfm/in-the-news?ID=3FD6EA53-802A-23AD-4FC1-A0F894986E81

[6] http://www.casey.senate.gov/newsroom/releases/senators-casey-sessions-and-clinton-applaud-passage-of-their-legislation-to-protect-bonuses-for-wounded-veterans

[7] https://www.govtrack.us/congress/bills/110/s2400

[8] http://washington.cbslocal.com/2013/09/11/jeb-bush-awards-hillary-clinton-liberty-medal/

[9] http://www.nytimes.com/2012/07/01/magazine/hillary-clintons-last-tour-as-a-rock-star-diplomat.html?pagewanted=all&_r=0

## 50. She Knows How to Negotiate

[1] http://www.huffingtonpost.com/entry/hillary-clinton-progressive_us_561dafabe4b050c6c4a35c32

[2] http://www.nytimes.com/2012/11/22/world/middleeast/israel-gaza-conflict.html

[3] http://time.com/2969852/hillary-clinton-john-kerry-barack-obama-israel-hamas/

[4] http://www.state.gov/secretary/20092013clinton/rm/2012/11/201343.htm

[5] https://www.washingtonpost.com/opinions/why-accepting-the-iran-nuclear-deal-is-a-no-brainer/2015/08/13/06adba26-3c5c-11e5-b3ac-8a79bc44e5e2_story.html

[6] http://www.washingtontimes.com/news/2014/dec/3/hillary-clinton-smart-show-respect-even-enemies/

[7] http://www.state.gov/secretary/20092013clinton/rm/2011/12/179173.htm

[8] http://www.epw.senate.gov/public/index.cfm/in-the-news?ID=3FD6EA53-802A-23AD-4FC1-A0F894986E81

[9] http://www.casey.senate.gov/newsroom/releases/senators-casey-sessions-and-clinton-applaud-passage-of-their-legislation-to-protect-bonuses-for-wounded-veterans

## 51. She Is Unbreakable

[1] June 13, 2015, Roosevelt Island campaign rally. Full text: http://www.cnn.com/2015/06/13/politics/hillary-clinton-campaign-rally-full-transcript-2016/
[2] Clinton, Hillary Rodham, *Hard Choices* (New York: Simon & Schuster, 2014).[3]http://www.nytimes.com/2015/06/13/us/politics/story-of-hillary-clintons-mother-forms-emotional-core-of-campaign.html
[4] http://www.slate.com/articles/news_and_politics/politics/2015/10/hillary_clinton_won_the_benghazi_hearing.html
[5] http://www.foxnews.com/politics/2015/10/23/clinton-seeks-to-turn-page-on-benghazi-with-testimony-can/
[6] http://www.telegraph.co.uk/news/2013729/US-elections-How-Hillary-Clinton-beat-John-McCain-at-vodka-drinking.html
[7] http://www.buzzfeed.com/rubycramer/lgbt-issues-racism-immigration-hillary-clinton-pitches-herse#.bc12mPrWXb
[8] May 28, 2015: https://www.hillaryclinton.com/the-four-fights/strengthening-americas-families/

## 52. She Will Make America Whole

[1] http://www.dailykos.com/story/2016/2/27/1492599/-Hillary-Clinton-s-South-Carolina-speech-Transcript
[2] http://www.usmagazine.com/celebrity-news/news/donald-trumps-craziest-quotes-the-2016-presidential-hopeful-speaks-201568
[3] http://blogs.wsj.com/washwire/2015/07/13/hillary-clinton-transcript-building-the-growth-and-fairness-economy/
[4] http://time.com/3920332/transcript-full-text-hillary-clinton-campaign-launch/
[5] http://www.msnbc.com/rachel-maddow-show/still-waiting-gop-alternative-obamacare
[6] http://thinkprogress.org/lgbt/2014/12/04/3599517/enda-demise/
[7] http://www.foxnews.com/opinion/2015/10/20/dear-republicans-keep-your-hands-off-social-security.html